Gender Equality in
European Contract Law

Ruth Nielsen

Gender Equality in European Contract Law

DJØF Publishing Copenhagen
2004

Gender Equality in European Contract Law
First edition

Print: Holbæk Amts Bogtrykkeri, Holbæk
Binding: Damm's Forlagsbogbinderi, Randers

Printed in Denmark 2004
ISBN 87-574-0687-1

DJØF Publishing
17, Lyngbyvej
P.O.B. 2702
DK-2100 Copenhagen
Denmark

Phone: +45 39 13 55 00
Fax: +45 39 13 55 55
E-mail: forlag@djoef.dk
www.djoef.dk-forlag

Preface

In this book I discuss the gender mainstreaming strategy and the ban on sex discrimination in relation to European contract law and put the current debate on European contract law into a gender perspective.

Copenhagen, 8 March 2004   Ruth Nielsen

Abbreviations

AG	Advocate General
BGB	Bürgerliches Gesetzbuch (German Civil Code)
CEDAW	United Nation Convention on the Elimination of All Forms of Discrimination against Women
DG	Directorate General (in the Commission)
EC	European Community
ECJ	Court of Justice of the European Communities (established under the EC Treaty, sits in Luxembourg)
ECHR	European Convention for the Protection of Human Rights and Fundamental Freedoms (adopted within the framework of the Council of Europe in 1950)
ECtHR	European Court of Human Rights (established under ECHR, sits in Strasbourg)
ECR	European Court Reports
EEA	European Economic Area
EEC	European Economic Community (renamed EC by the Maastricht Treaty with effect from 1.11.1993)
EU	European Union
GG	Grundgesetz (German Constitution)
nyr	Not yet reported
OJ	Official Journal
SDA	Sex Discrimination Act 1975 (UK)
UK	United Kingdom

Citation of articles of the EC and EU Treaties are made in the following way: Where reference is made to an article of the EC Treaty or the EU Treaty, the number of the article is immediately followed by two letters indicating the Treaty concerned. Article 13 EC thus denotes Article 13 of the EC Treaty and Article 6 EU Article 6 of the EU Treaty. If nothing else is explicitly stated, references are made to the current numbers as they are after the renumbering of the Articles of the EC and EU Treaties by the Amsterdam Treaty with effect from 1.5.1999.

Contents

Chapter 1

Introduction

1. Aim of the book

In this book, I discuss the interaction of contract law and gender equality law. Seen from the point of view of gender equality law what is happening in this interaction is mainly an extension of the scope of gender equality law and its underlying concepts and principles from employment contracts to (nearly) all other types of contracts, in particular contracts for the provision of goods and services. Seen from the point of view of contract law what is happening is both a limitation of the principle of freedom of contract for the parties to (private) contracts and of the autonomy of the Member States as a consequence of increased EU intervention based on a concern for equality as a fundamental human right.

In this book I focus on the gender mainstreaming strategy and the ban on sex discrimination in relation to European contract law and put the current debate on European contract law[1] into a gender perspective. The book brings together the dispersed pieces of law which deal with gender equality in matters of contract and discusses the potential in the equality provisions in the draft Constitutional Treaty[2] and the proposed Article 13 Directive[3] on equal treatment in the provision of goods and services. The concept of contract law is used in a broad sense, see further in chapter 4.

---

[1] See on this debate COM(2003)68 'A More Coherent European Contract Law - an Action Plan', see further DG SANCO's contract law website at europa.eu.int/comm/consumers/cons_int/safe_shop/fair_bus_pract/cont_law/index_en.htm and DG Markt's contract law website at europa.eu.int/comm/internal_market/contract law/index_en.htm. See on the academic debate Grundmann, Stefan and Jules Stuyck (eds): An Academic Green paper on European Contract Law, Kluwer Law international 2002 with further references and for more details below in Chapter 6.

[2] Available at european-convention.eu.int/docs/Treaty/CV00528.EN03.pdf.

[3] COM(2003)657, Proposal for a Council Directive implementing the principle of equal treatment between women and men in the access to and supply of goods and services. SEC(2003)1213, Commission Staff Working Paper contains an Extended Impact Assessment of the proposal.

2. Extension of Experiences from Employment Contract Law

Within existing contract law the gender equality aspect has so far been taken most seriously into account in the area of employment and occupation where abundant legislation, case law and literature,[4] both at national and EU level, have emerged during the last 20-30 years.

In this book, I draw on the experiences gained in the field of employment, in particular in respect of the basic concepts and methods, but as regards substantive law the focus is on matters other than employment,[5] ie broadly the subject matter covered by the proposed Directive on equal treatment between women and men in the provision of goods and services. Many of the examples of discrimination in the provision of goods and services reported in the preparatory material underlying the proposal consist in banks and other financial institutions committing more or less the same forms of sex discrimination in respect of credit facilities and access to capital as employers have practised in the employment field over a number of years. The abundant case law restricting sex discrimination by employers can, once the proposed Directive is adopted, be used by analogy against financial institutions.

As regards equal treatment for women-owned or women-led businesses the proposed directive can be seen as a reinforcement and further development of the already existing directive on the application of the principle of equal treatment between men and women engaged in an activity, including agriculture, in a self-employed capacity, and on the protection of self-employed women during pregnancy and motherhood. Equal access to set up a business, including equal access to financial services, is already provided for in that directive.[6]

There is an opposite historical sequence in the development of EU contract law and national contract law. In national contract law general contract law was developed first while a number of special contracts, for example employment contracts, were subjected to specific regulation more recently. In contrast, EU

---

[4] See for an overview europa.eu.int/comm/employment_social/equ_opp/ rights_en.html, see also Nielsen, Ruth: European Labour Law, Copenhagen 2000 Chapter V with further references.

[5] The communication COM (2001)398 with which the Commission launched the current debate on European contract law also left employment contracts out.

[6] 86/613/EEC, see in particular Article 4 which provides: 'As regards self-employed persons, Member States shall take the measures necessary to ensure the elimination of all provisions which are contrary to the principle of equal treatment as defined in Directive 76/207/EEC, especially in respect of the establishment, equipment or extension of a business or the launching or extension of any other form of self-employed activity including financial facilities.'

16

contract law started with specific contracts, with employment contract law as an early and well-developed area, and has not yet (fully) arrived at the traditional core issues of contract law. This context implies that experiences gained in employment contract law may be utilized in developing general contract law doctrines.

In the 1990's one-in-twelve of all Article 234 EC references from national courts to the ECJ for a preliminary ruling concerned sex discrimination (in employment)[7] which is one of the areas where the judicial dialogue between national courts and the ECJ has been most intense.[8] The ECJ has used sex discrimination cases as starting points for discovering and developing basic principles of EU law, such as for example directly binding horizontal effect *viz a viz* private individuals, duty to interpret national law in conformity with directives and state liability. The principle of equality between men and women[9] has been elevated into a fundamental right and a general principle of EU law.

At legislative level in the EU, employment sex discrimination law has served as a model for EU discrimination law more generally. In 2000, a Directive on Racial Discrimination[10] in all areas covered by EU law and a Framework Employment Directive for combatting discrimination on grounds of religion or belief, disability, age or sexual orientation[11] were adopted. These directives are heavily inspired by the experiences gained in the field of sex discrimination in employment. The Race Discrimination Directive covers both employment and occupation and a number of areas outside of the labour market, including access to and supply of goods and services. In 2002, the Employment and Occupation

---

[7] See further Sweet, Alec Stone and Thomas Brunell: The European Court, National Judges and Legal Integration, in Europarättslig Tidskrift 2000 p 179.

[8] Kilpatrick, Claire: Gender Equality: A Fundamental Dialogue in Sciarra, Silvana (ed): Labour law in the courts - National judges and the European Court of Justice, Hart Publishing, Oxford, 2001, contains a comparative analysis of the judicial dialogue which over the years has been conducted between the ECJ and the courts in 6 EU Member States: Denmark, France, Germany, Italy, Spain and the United Kingdom on gender equality law. She divides the 6 Member States under examination into three couples according to their level of preliminary reference activity. The most active couple is Germany and the UK, followed by France and Denmark who referred later, less and on fewer issues. Spain and Italy make up an inactive couple with no decided references on January 1, 2001.

[9] Case 149/77 *Defrenne* (No 3) [1978] ECR 1365.

[10] 2000/43/EC, proposal in COM(1999) 566, amended proposal COM(2000) 328.

[11] 2000/78/EC, COM(1999) 565.

Directive[12] on Equal Treatment between Men and Women was amended to consolidate the practice of the ECJ and to align it with the definitions of basic concepts used in the above directives on discrimination on grounds of race, etc.

With the proposal for a Directive on equal treatment between women and men in the provision of goods and services from November 2003, which was prepared by DG Employment, the Commission is continuing this practice of building on experiences from sex discrimination in employment when developing discrimination law in other areas. Many provisions of the proposed contract law directive on equal treatment in the access to and supply of goods and services[13] are word-by-word identical with provisions in the amended Equal Treatment Directive from 2002.[14]

There are prohibitions against discrimination and/or restrictions of free movement on grounds of nationality in Articles 12 EC (general prohibition), 28 EC (goods), 39 EC (workers), 43 EC (freedom of establishment), 49 EC (services) and 56 EC (capital). In *Angonese*,[15] which was a case about free movement of workers, the ECJ held that Articles 12 and 39 EC are directly binding for private persons.

Parties to private contracts are thus already under existing law prevented from discriminating on grounds of nationality. In January 2004, the Commission presented a draft proposal for a Directive on Services which contains more detailed provisions on discrimination/restrictions on grounds of nationality.[16] The current definition of indirect discrimination (in all areas of law) is inspired

---

[12] 2002/73/EC amending directive 76/207/EEC.

[13] COM(2003)657.

[14] 2002/73/EC.

[15] Case C-281/98, *Angonese* [2000] ECR I-4139. See, in particular, paragraph 35. The Court stated, after referring to Case 43/75, *Defrenne* [1976] ECR 455, paragraph 31: '35. Such considerations must, *a fortiori*, be applicable to Article 48 [now 39] of the Treaty, which lays down a fundamental freedom and which constitutes a specific application of the general prohibition of discrimination contained in Article 6 of the EC Treaty (now, after amendment, Article 12 EC)....'

[16] Article 21 of the proposed directive provides: 'Non-discrimination. 1. Member States shall ensure that the recipient is not subjected to discriminatory requirements based on his nationality or place of residence.' The proposal is available at europa.eu.int/comm/internal_market/en/services/services/docs/2004-proposal_en.pdf. It is provisional and subject to further linguistic revisions.

by the case law of the ECJ in cases involving the free movement of workers, see further below in Chapter 3.[17]

3. Is Gender Equality a Problem in Contracts for the Provision of Goods and Services?

Most businesses practising customers relations management (CRM), market segmentation and similar business strategies think of actual and potential customers as belonging to groups characterised by demographic data such as age and gender and a number of more individual personal data, see further below in Chapter 3 on the question as to whether market segmentation by gender constitutes direct or indirect sex discrimination within the meaning of gender equality law.

The scale of the problem of sex discrimination in the area of goods and services is difficult to assess. This is in part because, by definition, no record of complaints of sex discrimination are kept in Member States which have no specific legislation in the field – discrimination as an unlawful act only exists once it is prohibited. The Commission Staff Working Paper[18] supporting the proposal for a Directive on equal treatment in the provision of goods and services quotes a Eurobarometer survey carried out in 2002, where people saying that they had personally experienced discrimination on grounds of sex in the area of goods and services made up just under one quarter of the discrimination reported in this area on all grounds covered by the survey.[19]

In Member States where legislation prohibiting sex discrimination in the provision of goods and services does exist, complaints in the area of goods and services make up a significant proportion of those dealt with by the specialised bodies concerned. In Ireland, for example, the proportion of sex discrimination cases dealt with in 2003[20] by the Office for the Director of Equality Investigations concerning goods and services represented approximately 25% (with the remaining 75% concerning employment).

---

[17] See in particular Case C-237/94 *O'Flynn* [1996] ECR 2417.

[18] SEC(2003)1213.

[19] Other grounds included racial and ethnic origin, religion and belief, disability, age and sexual orientation.

[20] Before the publication on 10.11.2003 of the above Working Paper SEC(2003)1213.

3.1. Isolated instances of sex discrimination

Isolated instances of sex discrimination (direct or indirect discrimination, harassment or sexual harassment) probably occur in all areas of contract law and at all stages of the contractual process. In many member states such behaviour is already unlawful in a number of situations, see for an overview Chapter 2. When (and if) the draft Constitution and/or the proposed directive on equal treatment in the access to and supply of goods and services are adopted the existing prohibition against discrimination on grounds of sex in matters of contract law will be reinforced, extended and generalised to the whole of EU.

3.2. Discriminatory practices

In the proposal[21] for a directive on equal treatment in the provision of goods and services from November 2003 discriminatory practices operated by members of the business community are considered to be particularly widespread in financial services and in the portrayal of women in advertising and the media.

3.2.1. ICT and media sectors

It is generally the ambition of the European Union to become the most competitive and dynamic knowledge-based economy in the world, capable of sustainable economic growth with more and better jobs. At almost the same time as the Commission[22] adopted its proposal for a Directive on equal treatment in the provision of goods and services the Council[23] adopted a resolution on equal access to and participation of women and men in the knowledge society for growth and innovation. In this Resolution the Council recognizes the important role that gender equality can play in the context of developing a competitive and dynamic knowledge-based economy. It invites the Member States to foster greater participation of women in research-based activities and businesses, as a tool for enhancing innovation and to encourage the creation and ongoing development of enterprises by women, as well as the equal participation of men and women in policy and decision making in the ICT and media sectors.

In spite of the above focus on ICT and media as important vehicles for gender equality in the knowledge-based society, the Commission in the proposal for a Directive on equal treatment in the access to and supply of goods and services gave in to resistance to the proposal from the media sectors. The Commission

---

[21] See further COM(2003)657 and the underlying SEC(2003)1213.

[22] COM(2003)657 was presented 5.11.2003.

[23] Council Resolution of 27.11.2003 on equal access to and participation of women and men in the knowledge society for growth and innovation, OJ 2003 C 317.

states that many stakeholders think that the portrayal of women in the media and advertising poses serious questions about the protection of the dignity of men and women.[24] Representatives of the media argued that an attempt to regulate the content of the media would constitute an infringement of media freedoms. To avoid conflict with other fundamental freedoms, the proposed directive does not apply to the content of media and advertising.

The borderline between advertising and contractual statements may be blurred. It is for example sometimes questionable whether a statement in an advertisement is a binding offer. According to the Consumer Sales Directive[25] advertising is to be taken into account when deciding the content of a guarantee and whether goods are in conformity with the contract. The problems the proposed directive may pose in drawing the line between contractual statements which must abide by the principle of gender equality and advertisements which the proposed directive leaves free to discriminate on grounds of sex are discussed below in Chapter 4.

3.2.2. Insurance

It is common for insurance - especially life, health and car insurance and the calculation of annuities - to be offered on different terms to women and to men. Article 4 of the proposed directive on equal treatment in the access to and supply of goods and services specifically targets this problem by prohibiting the use of sex as a factor in the calculation of premiums and benefits for the purpose of insurance and related financial services in all new contracts, see further below in Chapter 4.

In some EU countries a number of social, health and educational services are mainly provided by the (welfare) state. There seems to be a tendency towards increased privatization whereby public law solutions are supplemented by or replaced by private contract law solutions.

Historically, the gender equality principle has been established earlier and more firmly in public law than in contract law. In the proposal for a Directive on equal treatment in the provision of goods and services the Commission argues[26] that the move towards private provision of services is undermining the principle of gender equality in that sex-neutrality in state social insurance schemes is being gradually replaced by sex differentiation in the private market. If privatization shall be possible without lowering the standard of gender equality

---

[24] COM(2003)657 p 5.

[25] 1999/44/EC on certain aspects of the sale of consumer goods and associated guarantees.

[26] COM(2003)657 p 8.

contract law, in particular in relation to insurance and pension contracts, must ensure the same level of gender equality as public law.

3.2.3. Access to Venture Capital

Research from the US suggests that there is a funding gap in women-led ventures. In a report on the Diana project[27] it is stated that (emphasis added):

> In 2000, estimates were that women owned *38 percent* of all businesses in the U.S., or roughly 9 million businesses. ... The reported numbers suggest that between 1953 and 1998, venture capital financing went to approximately 7,916 male-led businesses and 395 female-led businesses (*4.8 percent* of the total). Further breakdown of these numbers reveals that in 1997, the proportion of deals going to women-led firms was *2.5 percent* with a substantial increase to *5 percent* in 2001.

Article 5 of the proposed directive on equal treatment in the provision of goods and services allows positive action. In the explanatory remarks to this provision, the Commission mentions women's difficulty in raising venture capital as a reason why positive action for women businesses may be upheld or introduced.[28]

3.2.4. Access to Credit Facilities

Historically men and women have not had the same access to credit. Both women lenders and women burrowers have by and large been confined to small-scale credit.[29]

In present day society many instances of sex discrimination in connection with credit are still reported. In the Staff Working Paper[30] on the proposed directive on equal treatment in the access to and supply of goods and services the following examples (from the UK and Ireland) are mentioned:

> Refusal to provide a mortgage to pregnant women.
> Refusal to offer loans to people working part-time

---

[27] The Diana Project. Women business owners and equity capital: the myths dispelled, at www.entreworld.org/Bookstore/PDFs/RE-032.pdf. See generally on the Diana project www.esbri.se/diana.asp.

[28] COM(2003)657 p 14.

[29] See further Lemire, Beverly, Ruth Pearson and Gail Campbell (eds): Women and credit - Researching the past, refiguring the future, Oxford, 2002. In pre-industrial society women made the majority of pawn-transactions, see Lemire, Beverly: Introduction. Women, Credit and the Creation of Opportunity: A Historical Overview, op cit p 9.

[30] SEC(2003)1213 p 7.

Requirement for a woman to have a guarantor for a loan, where a man with a similar credit rating would not face a similar requirement.

An analysis of the Danish Agency for Trade and Industry published in 2000 revealed a number of barriers for women entrepreneurs' access to bank loans in the starting phase of a business, see further below in Chapter 4. One of the respondents stated:[31]

'Single mothers do not have much chance of obtaining a loan for their enterprises.'

The respondents in the analysis were staff in the banks and independent advisors to the banks, eg chartered accountants, ie representatives of or advisers to the potential discriminators and not representatives of potential victims.

As mentioned, Article 5 of the proposed directive on equal treatment in the provision of goods and services allows for positive action. In the explanatory remarks to this provision, the Commission mentions specific loans for women entrepreneurs, at special rates or conditions, and the provision of extra business support and advice services for women entrepreneurs as possible means of overcoming the accumulated disadvantage faced by women in this area.[32]

3.2.5. Consumer Surety Contracts

A consumer surety is often a woman, either a wife who stands surety for her husband or an elderly mother who stands surety for her son. A typical function of a consumer surety contract is to transfer money from women to men. The issue of surety wives and their legal position has been addressed in legal literature[33] and case law on a number of occasions during recent years. In Royal Bank of Scotland v Etridge (AP) the House of Lords set out procedures to be followed by lenders in order to counter any argument by the wife that the contract should be set aside because her signature has been obtained by the

---

[31]   The Relations of Banks to Women Entrepreneurs. The Analysis of the Danish Agency for Trade and Industry: Women Entrepreneurs Now and in the Future, Published by the Danish Agency for Trade and Industry, September 2000, available online at www.efs.dk/publikationer/rapporter/bankers.uk/index-eng.html. The quotation on single mothers is from part 2.2.

[32]   COM(2003)657 p 14.

[33]   See for example Fehlberg, Belinda: Sexually transmitted debt - Surety experience and English law, Oxford 1997, Morris, Debra: Surety Wives in the House of Lords: Time for Solicitors to 'Get Real'? Royal Bank of Scotland plc v Etridge (No 2) [2001] 4 All ER 449, Feminist Legal Studies 2003 p 57 and Geary, David: Notes on Family Guarantees in English and Scottish Law - A Comment, European Review of Private Law 2000 p 25.

undue influence of her husband. The House of Lords held that whenever the relationship between the debtor and surety is a 'non-commercial' one, such as when a wife offers to stand surety for her husband's debts the wife should receive independent advice.[34]

The proposal for a Directive on credit for consumers from 2002,[35] which for the first time will harmonise the law on consumer surety contracts, does, however, not, in spite of the gender mainstreaming duty of all EU actors, integrate the gender aspect, see further below in Chapter 3 and 4. Women's surety obligations may give rise to over-indebtedness and gender specific patterns in bankruptcy.[36]

4. Comparative Perspective with focus on EU Law

In this book, I look at contract law in a comparative perspective with the focus on EU Law. The classic role of comparative law is to compare legal systems of different countries. Due to the cross-fertilization of EU law and the national laws of the EU countries comparative law is in the process of taking over a new dimension and becomes a tool to enable harmonization between the national legals systems within the EU and to maintain or obtain coherence within and between the national and EU legal order.[37] For comparative purposes the EU countries may be divided into 3 groups:[38]

- the common law system (UK and Ireland)
- the Nordic system (Denmark, Finland and Sweden)

---

[34] www.parliament.the-stationery-office.co.uk/pa/ld200102/ldjudgmt/d011011/et ridg-1.htm, 11 October 2001 [2001] UKHL 44.

[35] COM(2002)443. Proposal for a Directive of the European Parliament and of the Council on the harmonisation of the laws, regulations and administrative provisions of the Member States concerning credit for consumers.

[36] See further Warren, Elizabeth: What is a Women's Issue? Bankruptcy, Commercial Law, and Other Gender-Neutral Topics, Harvard Women's Law Journal, 2002 p 19.

[37] Cf Walter van Gerven: Comparative Law in a Texture of Communitarization of National laws and Europeanization of Community Law, in O'Keeffe, David and Bavasso, Antonio (eds): Judicial Review in European Union Law, The Hague 2000 p 433.

[38] See generally Zweigert, Konrad and Hein Kötz: An Introduction to Comparative Law, Oxford 1998.

- the Romano-Germanic system (Austria, Germany, France, Belgium, Holland, Luxembourg, Spain, Portugal, Italy and Greece and the central and eastern European countries which will enter as of 1.5.2004)

EU labour law, which as mentioned has served as a model for the proposed directive on equal treatment in the provision of goods and services, is generally strongly inspired by the continental legal tradition.[39] Discrimination law is, however, more than other aspects of labour law influenced by common law. The concept of indirect sex discrimination in employment was developed in UK law before it was spread around the EU through EU legislation.[40] The concept of indirect sex discrimination in contract law in general is likely to enter the contract law of many civil law countries through the same route. First, it was provided for in the UK Sex Discrimination Act in 1975 and some 30 years later the proposed Directive on equal treatment in the access to and supply of goods and services will (if adopted) introduce the concept of indirect discrimination in the provision of goods and services into the remaining EU countries and further develop it in those countries where it already forms part of current law.

5. A Multi-Layered View of Gender Equality in Contract Law

5.1. The surface level, the legal culture and the deep structure

Tuori[41] has argued that law and its changes should be examined on three levels: the surface level of the law; the legal culture; and the deep structure of law.

The surface level of the law comprises various pieces of legislation as well as court and administrative decisions in individual cases. Standpoints in legal dogmatical writing are also placed at this level.

---

[39] See further Nielsen, Ruth: European Labour Law, Copenhagen 2000.

[40] Dockès, Emmanuel: Equality in Labour Law: An Economically Efficient Human Right? Reflections from a French Law Perspective, International Journal of Comparative Labour Law and Industrial Relations 2002 p 187 states: 'Indirect discrimination has come to France from the Anglo-Saxon legal cultures via the case-law of the ECJ and, more recently, EU directives. See on the common law influence in employment discrimination law Thüsing, Gregor: Following the US Example: European Employment Discrimination Law and the Impact of Council Directives 2000/43/EC and 2000/78/EC, International Journal of Comparative Labour Law and Industrial Relations 2003 p 187.

[41] See further on the levels of law Tuori, Kaarlo: Critical Legal Positivism,Aldershot 2002 chapter 6. See also Tuori, Kaarlo: Towards a Multi-Layered View ofModern Law, in Aarnio, Aulis et al (eds): Justice, Morality and Society, Lund 1997.

The legal culture constitutes the middle or mediating level of law. One may distinguish between the expert legal culture and the general legal culture of ordinary citizens. The expert legal culture includes the general principles of law and its basic concepts as well as various rules used in interpreting norms (such as analogy and *e contrario*) and solving norm conflicts (such as *lex superior, lex specialis* and *lex posterior*). In addition, a central element of the expert legal culture consists of patterns of argumentation.

Tuori uses the term deep structure of law to name the common core of a distinct historical type of law, eg modern law. This is the most inert part of law as to its development and change. EU law represents a late stage in the stabilisation of modern law (and not the emergence of post-modern law).[42]

Viewed in this way, the legal development starts at the surface level and then gradually over a number of years settles down as deeper layers of law. Legal history is thus a process of sedimentation. Young legal orders - like EU contract law and gender equality law - are generally more superficial than old legal systems. The interaction (sedimentation, constitution, specification, limitation, justification and criticism)[43] of the different levels of law has different consequences for the visibility of the gender dimension in contract law.

5.2. Law as a legal order and as legal practices

Contract law can be seen as a legal order, ie a set of legal norms, and as legal practices. In this book I will look at gender equality in contracting in both ways. As regards legal practices I will focus on legislative practice, adjudication and legal science.

Generally, I think it is the primary task of legal science to develop the law as a system, in particular its basic concepts and general principles.[44] In this book, it is my aim to contribute to clarifying the relevant concepts related to gender equality in contract law and to establishing the principle of equal treatment between men and women as a general principle of contract law.

---

[42] Tuori, Kaarlo: EC Law: An Independent Legal Order or a Post-Modern Jack-in-the-Box? in I. Cameron and A. Simoni (eds) Dealing with Integration, vol 2, Perspectives from seminars on European Law 1996-1998 p 225 et seq, Uppsala 1998.

[43] See further Tuori, Kaarlo: Critical Legal Positivism, Aldershot 2002 chapter 7.

[44] See for a similar view Wilhelmsson, Thomas: Social Contract Law and European Integration, Dartmouth 1995.

5.3. The (in)visibility of the gender dimension

In contract law the gender dimension is much more visible at the surface level of the law than in the underlying sub-surface layers of the legal culture and the deep structure of law.

In many EU countries there is national legislation explicitly prohibiting discrimination in contractual relations and all EU countries have adhered to CEDAW,[45] see further below in Chapter 2. In addition, the pending EU proposals (the draft Constitution and the proposed Directive on equal treatment in the provision of goods and services) will lay down general principles providing a common minimum level of gender equality protection. The surface level of contract law governing gender equality consequently consists of different layers originating from national and supra-national sources.

Within legal practices (legislative practice, adjudication and legal science) the gender-dimension is particularly visible in legislative practice. In addition, there is some case law, in particular in the UK where the Sex Discrimination Act which prohibits sex discrimination in the provision of goods and services dates back to 1975. In mainstream scholarly writing on contract law the gender dimension is by and large not explicitly integrated.

6. From an Internal Market to a Fundamental Rights Perspective

At EU level, the problems discussed in this book are mainly interesting in two different contexts: an internal market and a fundamental rights perspective. Gender-related contractual behaviour and fragmentary legal regulation of it varying from country to country may cause obstacles to the free movement on the internal market. If, for example, the premium in a contract for life insurance can lawfully be based on sex-related actuarial factors in one Member State but not in another the free movement of that service will be hindered.

In addition, equal treatment between women and men is a fundamental right. In the proposal for a Directive on equal treatment in the access to and supply of goods and services,[46] the Commission explicitly stresses that the EU approach to gender equality has developed over time, so that the original emphasis on equal pay and on avoiding distortions of competition between Member States has been replaced by a concern for equality as a fundamental right.

A similar development has taken place in case law. The ECJ has, since the ruling in *Defrenne* (3) in 1978, considered equality between men and women a

---

[45] United Nation's Convention on the Elimination of All Forms of Discrimination against Women, available at www.un.org/womenwatch/daw/cedaw/.

[46] COM(2003)657 p 2.

fundamental right and a general principle of law.[47] In 1976, in *Defrenne* (2),[48] the ECJ took the view, as regards Article 141 EC on equal pay, that it pursues a twofold purpose, both economic and social. In *Schröder,*[49] the ECJ went further and held that the economic goals of avoiding distortion of competition underlying Article 141 EC are secondary to the social aims of that provision, which constitutes the expression of a fundamental human right.

In this book, I discuss the implications for European contract law of applying either an internal market or a fundamental rights perspective and in that context look across the divide between public law and private law.

---

[47] Case 149/77, *Defrenne* (No 3) [1978] ECR 1365.

[48] Case 43/75, *Defrenne* (No 2) [1976] ECR 455 paragraph 8-11.

[49] Case C-50/96, *Schröder* [2000] ECR I-743 paragraph 57.

Chapter 2

Sources of Law

1. Introduction

In this chapter I highlight the changes in the general pattern of the sources of contract law the increasing - to a high degree EU driven - regulation of gender equality in contract matters is resulting in. I examine where in the legal system and at what level in the hierarchy of the sources of law rules on gender equality in contract matters outside of employment are (being) placed. Gender equality rules have so far mainly entered the contract law system(s) through two routes:

1) via mandatory gender-specific legislation at national, EU and international level, and
2) as a fundamental right and general principle of EU law.

From a quantitative point of view, most of the rules on gender equality in the contract law currently in force are found in mandatory gender-specific legislation at national level. When (and if) the pending proposal[1] for a Directive on equal treatment in the provision of goods and services is adopted the prohibition against discrimination on grounds of sex in contract law which already exists in a number of Member States will be reinforced, extended and generalised to the whole of EU and elevated to EU level.

Gender equality is a fundamental right and a general principle of EU law which is applicable both in EU law, including EU contract law, and in national contract law in areas covered by Community law, eg national legislation implementing the consumer law directives. The fundamental right and general principle of gender equality is enshrined in the draft Constitution for the EU which once adopted will strengthen the constitutional dimension of both national and EU contract law.

So far, the gender dimension is only to a very limited extent integrated into the mainstream sources of contract law (gender-neutral legislation, national case law and academic writing). It also plays only a minor role in the current debate on European contract law. The gender mainstreaming strategy (see below in

---

[1] COM(2003)756.

Chapter 3) has thus not (yet) been successfully applied in respect of sources of gender equality in contract law.

2. Mandatory Gender Specific Legislation

The 1990's saw high legislative activity at both EU and national level relating to the promotion of equality and elimination of discrimination between men and women.

2.1. The EC Treaty

Important provisions on gender equality were inserted into the EC Treaty by the Amsterdam Treaty which came into force 1.5.1999. Before that date there was only one article in the EC Treaty dealing explicitly with gender equality, namely the equal pay provision in the then Article 119 [now after amendment Article 141 EC]. In the Amsterdam version of the EC Treaty there are 5 articles dealing explicitly with gender equality, two of which (Article 137 EC and Article 141 EC) are concerned with employment and occupation.

With the adoption of the Amsterdam Treaty EU gender equality law grew out of the confines of employment law. Three of the new gender equality provisions (Article 2 EC, Article 3(2) EC and Article 13 EC) govern all areas under Community competence, including *inter alia* contract law in matters other than employment and occupation.

2.1.1. Promoting equality is a task of the EU
By the Amsterdam Treaty the objectives of the Community were widened. Article 2 EC[2] lists 10 objectives, one of which is to promote equality between women and men. Promotion of gender equality is thus one of the objectives of EU contract law. The objectives of Community law are of great importance because the ECJ applies a teleological method of interpretation and puts a

---

[2]   Article 2 EC reads (emphasis added): 'The Community shall have as its *task*, by establishing a common market and an economic and monetary union and by implementing common policies or activities referred to in Articles 3 and 4, *to promote* throughout the Community a harmonious, balanced and sustainable development of economic activities, a high level of employment and of social protection, *equality between men and women*, sustainable and non-inflationary growth, a high degree of competitiveness and convergence of economic performance, a high level of protection and improvement of the quality of the environment, the raising of the standard of living and quality of life, and economic and social cohesion and solidarity among Member States.' Under Article 3 of the Draft Constitutional Treaty (available at european-convention.eu.int/docs/Treaty/CV00528. EN03.pdf) it is one of the objectives of the Union to promote equality between women and men.

meaning upon Community law - also older elements thereof - that is in accordance with the objectives at the time of interpretation, see for example AG Stix-Hackl's interpretation in *Dory*[3] where she argued that the old Equal Treatment Directive from 1976,[4] after the Amsterdam Treaty, should be interpreted in the light of the mainstreaming provision in Article 3(2) EC and therefore could not be construed as having a narrow scope of application. See also *Allonby*,[5] discussed below.

2.1.2. Gender mainstreaming

One of the innovative features of the 3rd Action Programme for Equality 1991-1995 was to put the mainstreaming strategy on the Community agenda. The later Action Programmes for Equality strengthened this strategy. The mainstreaming strategy was reinforced by the Amsterdam Treaty which elevated it in the hierarchy of the sources of law from soft law to Treaty level. Article 3(2) EC now provides that in all the activities referred to in that Article, the Community shall aim to eliminate inequalities, and to promote equality, between men and women.[6] There is thus a duty upon all Community actors, including the national courts in their capacity as Community courts, not only to combat sex discrimination but to aim at eliminating inequalities and promoting equality, see further below in Chapter 3.

2.1.3. Legal base of ban on sex discrimination in contract law

As regards gender equality in contract law outside of employment and occupation the legal basis for binding Community legislation was weak before the coming into force of the Amsterdam Treaty when that situation was changed. Article 13 EC[7] - which is the legal base of the proposed Directive on equal

---

[3]   Case C-186/01, *Dory* [2003] ECR I-2479, paragraph 102-105.

[4]   76/207/EEC.

[5]   Case C-256/01, *Allonby* [2004] ECR I-0000 (nyr, judgment of 13.1.2004).

[6]   In the draft Constitutional Treaty Article 3(2) EC is replaced by Article II-23 (see below)and Article III-3 which puts an obligation upon the Member States to integrate the aim to combat discrimination based on sex, racial or ethnic origin, religion or belief, disability, age or sexual orientation when defining and implementing all the policies and activities referred to in Part III of the draft Constitution.

[7]   Article 13 EC provides: 'Without prejudice to the other provisions of this Treaty and within the limits of the powers conferred by it upon the Community, the Council, acting unanimously on a proposal from the Commission and after consulting the European Parliament, may take appropriate action to combat discrimination based on sex, racial or ethnic origin, religion or belief, disability, age or sexual orientation.'

treatment in the provision of goods and services - provides a clear legal basis for measures to combat sex discrimination. The appropriate action that can be taken under Article 13 EC includes all kinds of binding secondary EU legislation such as regulations and directives.

Article 13 only confers power on the EU legislator to adopt measures to combat discrimination. There seems to be no legal basis in Article 13 EC for binding secondary legislation providing for more wide-ranging gender mainstreaming measures. The Council has for example adopted a Resolution,[8] ie a piece of EU soft law which doesn't require any particular legal basis, on equal access to and participation of women and men in the knowledge society. As the law stands at present, and that will not be changed by the Constitutional Treaty,[9] the EU does probably not have power under Article 13 EC to adopt binding legislation providing for parity participation.

2.2. The proposed Directive on equal treatment in contracts for the provision of goods and services

2.2.1. Background

In its Social Policy Agenda from June 2000,[10] the Commission announced its intention to present a proposal for a directive to prohibit sex discrimination outside of the labour market to be based on Article 13 EC.

In November 2003, the Commission finally presented a proposal for a Directive implementing the principle of equal treatment between women and men in the access to and supply of goods and services.[11] Contracts for the access to and supply of (sale, etc) goods and services form a typical subject of contract law. The proposed Directive contains a horizontal prohibition of sex discrimina-

---

[8] OJ 2003 C 317, Council Resolution of 27 November 2003 on equal access to and participation of women and men in the knowledge society for growth and innovation.

[9] In the draft Constitutional Treaty Article 13 EC is replaced by Article III-8 which provides '1. Without prejudice to the other provisions of the Constitution and within the limits of the powers conferred by it upon the Union, a European law or framework law of the Council of Ministers may establish the measures needed to combat discrimination based on sex, racial or ethnic origin, religion or belief, disability, age or sexual orientation. The Council of Ministers shall act unanimously after obtaining the consent of the European Parliament.'

[10] COM(2000)379.

[11] COM(2003)657, Proposal for a Council Directive implementing the principle of equal treatment between women and men in the access to and supply of goods and services. SEC(2003)1213, Commission Staff Working Paper contains an Extended Impact Assessment of the proposal.

tion which will give legal form to the principle of gender equality in most areas of contract law.

2.2.2. Purpose

The proposed Directive lays down a framework for combatting sex discrimination in access to and supply of goods and services, with a view to putting into effect in the Member States the principle of equal treatment between men and women. The proposal for a Directive implements the principle of equal treatment in the field of the access to and supply of goods and services which are available to the public, including housing. In this respect, the Directive takes the same approach to the area as the Directive on Racial and Ethnic Discrimination.[12]

2.2.3. Definitions

The proposed Directive includes elaborate definitions of the concepts of direct and indirect discrimination, harassment and sexual harassment which are almost identical to the definitions adopted in 2002 in the amended Equal Treatment Directive.[13] Positive action, ie the maintenance and adoption of specific measures by Member States in a specific area will be allowed to overcome the weight of accumulated disadvantages linked to sex suffered by women or men see further below in Chapter 3.

2.2.4. Scope

Within the limits of the powers conferred upon the Community, the Directive shall apply to all persons in relation to the access to and the supply of goods and services which are available to the public, including housing, as regards both the public and private sectors, including public bodies, see further below in Chapter 4. The Directive does not preclude differences which are related to goods or services for which men and women are not in a comparable situation because the goods or services are intended exclusively or primarily for the members of one sex or to skills which are practised differently for each sex. The Directive shall not apply to education nor to the content of media and advertising.[14]

The proposed Directive specifically targets insurance and financial services and prohibits different treatment of men and women by reference to actuarial factors, see further below in Chapter 4.

---

[12] 2000/43/EC.

[13] 2002/73/EC amending Directive 76/207/EEC.

[14] In particular advertising and television advertising as defined in Article 1 (b) of Council Directive 89/552/EEC.

2.2.5. Remedies and enforcement machinery

The proposed Directive contains fairly elaborate provisions on remedies and enforcement, including the setting up of supervisory equality bodies and a rule shifting the burden of proof from the complainant to the respondent once the plaintiff has established facts before the court or other body from which it may be presumed that discrimination has taken place, see further below in Chapter 5.

2.3. Rules governing self-employed persons

2.3.1. Self-employed persons who are workers

The focus in this book is, as set out in Chapter 1, on matters other than employment. To some extent the EU employment provisions do, however, apply to contracts which the parties to the contracts - and also some national legal systems - regard as service contracts. This may be illustrated by the *Allonby* case.[15]

The situation in *Allonby* was that a college of further education in the UK terminated the employment of its part-time, mostly female lecturers. It subsequently bought in their services again through the intermediary of an agency with which those lecturers were registered as self-employed persons. Through this transformation of a predominantly female group of lecturers from employees into independent contractors the college sought to achieve savings in operating costs. For the lecturers concerned the change - from teaching under an employment contract to doing the same work under a service contract - entailed a diminution in pay. In that context a question[16] was referred to the ECJ as to whether the female lecturers concerned could demand admission to a pension scheme for teachers. As a precondition for membership of the pension scheme, set up by UK legislation, there was a requirement of being employed under a contract of employment. The question was whether such a requirement must be disapplied - because of the supremacy of EU law over UK law - where it is shown that, among the teachers who fulfil the other conditions for membership, a clearly lower percentage of women than of men are able to satisfy the condition of being employed under an employment contract (and not a service contract) and it is established that that condition is not objectively justified.

---

[15] Case C-256/01, *Allonby* [2004] ECR I-0000 (nyr, judgment of 13.1.2004).

[16] A number of other questions were also at issue in *Allonby*, see for example below in Chapter 3 on the requirement that a contested difference must stem from a single source.

The ECJ first pointed out that there is no single definition of worker in Community law: it varies according to the area in which the definition is to be applied.[17] The term worker within the meaning of Article 141(1) EC is not expressly defined in the EC Treaty. It is therefore necessary, in order to determine its meaning, to apply the generally recognised principles of interpretation, having regard to its context and to the objectives of the Treaty. According to Article 2 EC, the Community is to have as its task to promote, among other things, equality between men and women. Article 141(1) EC constitutes a specific expression of the principle of equality for men and women, which forms part of the fundamental principles protected by the Community legal order. The ECJ, in *Allonby*, reiterated that the principle of equal pay forms part of the foundations of the Community and stated:

Accordingly, the term worker used in Article 141(1) EC cannot be defined by reference to the legislation of the Member States but has a Community meaning. Moreover, it cannot be interpreted restrictively.

It is thus not up to neither the parties to the contract, nor the national legal system to decide the status of a person performing a service as either a worker or an independent contractor. If the performance of a particular service happens in such a way that the person performing the service comes under the wide Community concept of a worker Community law on gender equality in employment applies.

In conclusion, the ECJ answered the question as to whether the female lecturers concerned could demand admission to a pension scheme for teachers by stating (emphasis added) that Article 141(1) EC must be interpreted as meaning that in the absence of any objective justification, the requirement, imposed by State legislation, of being employed under a contract of employment as a precondition for membership of a pension scheme for teachers *is not applicable* [because of the supremacy of EU law over UK law] where it is shown that, among the teachers who are workers within the meaning of Article 141(1) EC and fulfil all the other conditions for membership, a much lower percentage of women than of men is able to fulfil that condition. The formal classification of a self-employed person under national law does not change the fact that a person must be classified as a worker within the meaning of that article if his independence is merely notional.

Women-owned businesses are often small businesses. In the analysis of the Danish Agency for Trade and Industry from 2000 on barriers for women

---

[17] Case C-85/96, *Martinez Sala* [1998] ECR I-2691, paragraph 31.

entrepreneurs' access to bank loans in the starting phase of a business[18] the fact that women entrepreneurs often apply for financing of small projects was mentioned as a reason why they were treated differently from male entrepreneurs with bigger plans. The fact that the Community concept of worker is broad entails that a number of service contracts concluded by small-businesses which are dependent on their contractual counterpart will be governed by the EU gender equality in employment rules.

2.3.2. Genuinely self-employed persons

As regards genuinely self-employed persons the proposed Directive on equal treatment in contracts for the provision of goods and services[19] can, as mentioned in Chapter 1, be seen as a reinforcement and further development of the already existing directive on the application of the principle of equal treatment between men and women engaged in an activity, including agriculture, in a self-employed capacity, and on the protection of self-employed women during pregnancy and motherhood.[20]

The purpose of that Directive is to ensure application in the Member States of the principle of equal treatment as between men and women engaged in an activity in a self-employed capacity, or contributing to the pursuit of such an activity, as regards those aspects not covered by earlier directives.[21] The Directive covers: (a) self-employed workers, ie all persons pursuing a gainful activity for their own account, under the conditions laid down by national law, including farmers and members of the liberal professions; (b) their spouses, not being employees or partners, where they habitually, under the conditions laid down by national law, participate in the activities of the self-employed worker and perform the same tasks or ancillary tasks.

For the purposes of the Directive the principle of equal treatment implies the absence of all discrimination on grounds of sex, either directly or indirectly, by reference in particular to marital or family status. Equal access to set up a

---

[18] The Relations of Banks to Women Entrepreneurs. The Analysis of The Danish Agency for Trade and Industry: Women Entrepreneurs now and in the Future, Published by the Danish Agency for Trade and Industry September 2000, available online at www.efs.dk/publikationer/ rappor ter/bankers.uk/index -e ng .h tm l.

[19] COM(2003)756.

[20] 86/613/EEC.

[21] 76/207/EEC and 79/7/EEC.

business, including equal access to financial services, is provided for in Article 4.[22]

2.4. The Draft Constitutional Treaty for the European Union

The Draft Constitutional Treaty for the European Union repeats the existing gender equality provisions in the EC Treaty with almost identical wording, see above on Article 2, 3 and 13 EC. The numbers of the Articles are changed and the terminology (European laws, European framework laws, European regulations, etc) in respect of secondary EU legislation is new.

In addition to upholding existing gender equality provisions in the EC Treaty equality is stated to be a value of the European Union.[23] According to Article 5(1) of the draft Constitutional Treaty, the Charter of Fundamental Rights from 2000[24] shall be an integral part of the Constitution. It will thus become legally binding, see below.

There is a Chapter on employment rights in the Charter but equality is placed in a chapter of its own thus consolidating the trend in the legislative development from the Amsterdam Treaty onwards to regulate equality matters independent of employment. There are rules on gender equality in Article II-21[25] and II-23[26] and on the reconciliation of professional and family life in Article II-33 of the Charter.

---

[22] Article 4 stipulates: 'As regards self-employed persons, Member States shall take the measures necessary to ensure the elimination of all provisions which are contrary to the principle of equal treatment as defined in Directive 76/207/EEC, especially in respect of the establishment, equipment or extension of a business or the launching or extension of any other form of self-employed activity including financial facilities.'

[23] Under Article 2 of the Draft Constitutional Treaty the Union is founded on the values of respect for human dignity, liberty, democracy, equality, the rule of law and respect for human rights. These values are declared to be common to the Member States in a society of pluralism, tolerance, justice, solidarity and non-discrimination.

[24] The EU Charter of Fundamental Rights was adopted as a soft law declaration at the Nice summit in December 2000.

[25] Article II-21(1) provides: Any discrimination based on any ground such as sex, race, colour, ethnic or social origin, genetic features, language, religion or belief, political or any other opinion, membership of a national minority, property, birth, disability, age or sexual orientation shall be prohibited.

[26] Article II-23 provides: Equality between men and women must be ensured in all areas, including employment, work and pay. The principle of equality shall not prevent the maintenance or adoption of measures providing for specific advantages in favour of the under-represented sex.

According to the preamble of the Charter as incorporated in the draft Constitutional Treaty the Charter will be interpreted by the courts of the Union and the Member States with due regard to the explanations[27] prepared at the instigation of the Praesidium of the Convention which drafted the Charter.

According to Article I-7 of the Draft Constitutional Treaty all citizens of the Union, women and men, shall be equal before the law. Article I-26(2) of the draft Constitution provides on the future composition of the Commission that each Member State shall establish a list of three persons, in which both genders shall be represented, whom it considers qualified to be a European Commissioner.

There is no protection of the principle of freedom of contract in the Charter of fundamental Rights. There is a provision in Article II-16 on freedom to conduct a business[28] and in Article II-17[29] on the right to property which may have some bearing on contract law.

Article 5(2) of the draft Constitutional Treaty provides a legal basis for EU accession to the ECHR, see further on ECHR below.

---

[27] http://register.consilium.eu.int/pdf/en/03/cv00/cv00828en03.pdf.

[28] Article 16 states: 'The freedom to conduct a business in accordance with Community law and national laws and practices is recognised.' In the explanatory remarks to this provision it is stated that it is based on ECJ case law which has recognised freedom to exercise an economic or commercial activity, see eg Case 4/73, *Nold* [1974] ECR 491.

[29] Article 17 states: '1. Everyone has the right to own, use, dispose of and bequeath his or her lawfully acquired possessions. No one may be deprived of his or her possessions, except in the public interest and in the cases and under the conditions provided for by law, subject to fair compensation being paid in good time for their loss. The use of property may be regulated by law in so far as is necessary for the general interest. 2. Intellectual property shall be protected.' In the explanatory remarks to this provision it is stated that it is a fundamental right common to all national constitutions. It has been recognised on numerous occasions by the case law of the ECJ, initially in case 44/79, *Hauer* ECR [1979] 3727. The wording has been updated but, in accordance with Article 52(3) of the Charter of fundamental rights, the meaning and scope of the right are the same as those of the right guaranteed by the ECHR and the limitations may not exceed those provided for there.

2.5. National Constitutions

In many EU Member States there are gender equality provisions in the Constitutions.[30] The existence of such provisions in many EU countries supports the view that gender equality is a fundamental right but it is unclear to what extent (if any) a contract law duty of equal treatment binding upon the parties (including private parties) to the contract can be derived from the constitutions in respect of other contracts than employment contracts.

The horizontal effect as between private parties of fundamental rights (Drittwirkung der Grundrechte) has played a particular role in German (labour) law. The German Constitutional Court (Bundesverfassungsgericht) stated in the Lüth case that:[31]

> 1. Die Grundrechte sind in erster Linie Abwehrrechte des Bürgers gegen den Staat; in den Grundrechtsbestimmungen des Grundgesetzes verkörpert sich aber auch eine objektive Wertordnung, die als verfassungsrechtliche Grundentscheidung für alle Bereiche des Rechts gilt.
> 2. Im bürgerlichen Recht entfaltet sich der Rechtsgehalt der Grundrechte mittelbar durch die privatrechtlichen Vorschriften. Er ergreift vor allem Bestimmungen zwingenden Charakters und ist für den Richter besonders realisierbar durch die Generalklauseln.

Article 3 of the German Grundgesetz (Constitution) provides:[32]

> (1) All humans are equal before the law.
> (2) Men and women are equal. The state supports the effective realization of equality of women and men and works towards abolishing present disadvantages.

---

[30] See Constitutions of Austria (Art 7.2), Belgium (Art 10.3, 10 bis), Finland (section 6-4), France (Preamble with constitutional value, Arts 3.5, 4.3), Germany (§3), Greece (Arts 4.2, 116.2), Ireland (Art 40), Italy (Art 51), Portugal (Art 9-h), Sweden (1st Chapter, Section 2.3).

[31] Available at www.oefre.unibe.ch/law/dfr/bv007198.html.

[32] Quoted from the English translation at www.oefre.unibe.ch/law/the_basic_law.pdf. The original reads: '(1) Alle Menschen sind vor dem Gesetz gleich. (2) Männer und Frauen sind gleichberechtigt. Der Staat fördert die tatsächliche Durchsetzung der Gleichberechtigung von Frauen und Männern und wirkt auf die Beseitigung bestehender Nachteile hin. (3) Niemand darf wegen seines Geschlechtes, seiner Abstammung, seiner Rasse, seiner Sprache, seiner Heimat und Herkunft, seines Glaubens, seiner religiösen oder politischen Anschauungen benachteiligt oder bevorzugt werden. Niemand darf wegen seiner Behinderung benachteiligt werden.'

(3) No one may be disadvantaged or favoured because of his sex, parentage, race, language, homeland and origin, his faith, or his religious or political opinions. No one may be disadvantaged because of his handicap.

It is usual to distinguish between direct horizontal effect (unmittelbare Drittwirkung) where the Constitution of itself creates rights and duties for private parties. Such effect is in German (labour) law only recognised in few cases, for example with regard to collective agreements. When the Constitution has indirect horizontal effect (mittelbare Drittwirkung) it operates between the parties through the medium of ordinary legislation which is interpreted so as to give effect to the fundamental right provided for in the Constitution. In German labour law the indirect horizontal effect of the Constitution plays a very important role.[33]

With regard to gender equality in matters outside of employment it is the general view that the above Art 3 GG has no direct horizontal effect (unmittelbare Drittwirkung) and it is a matter of dispute whether and to what extent it has indirect horizontal effect (mittelbare Drittwirkung). It is a widely shared assumption that freedom of contract and (mandatory) gender equality are irreconcilable. A leading commentary on the BGB states:[34]

'While civil law is governed by the principle of personal autonomy, it is impossible to derive a general obligation of equal treatment either from Article 3 GG (constitution) nor from para. 242 BGB (Civil Code)[35]'

The principle of freedom of contract is here seen as embodied in § 2 GG[36] and is interpreted as an overriding principle in collision with the principle of gender equality. Some authors differentiate between different aspects of Article 3 GG.

---

[33] See on 'Grundrechte im Arbeitsrecht' Gamillscheg, Franz: Arbeitsrecht I. Arbeitsvertrags- und Arbeitsschutzrecht, München 2001 p 50*et seq.*

[34] Palandt, Otto et al (eds), Bürgerliches Gesetzbuch, 2001, quoted from the translation in Schiek, Dagmar: Torn between Arithmetic and Substantive Equality? Perspectives on Equality in German Labour Law, The International Journal of Comparative Labour Law and Industrial Relations 2002 p 149. See for a critical viw on this position Schiek, Dagmar: Differenzierte Gerechtigkeit. Diskriminierungsschutz und Vertragsrecht, Baden-Baden 2000.

[35] BGB § 242 provides: 'Der Schuldner ist verpflichtet, die Leistung so zu bewirken, wie Treu und Glauben mit Rücksicht auf die Verkehrssitte es erfordern.'.

[36] § 2 I GG provides: '(1) Jeder hat das Recht auf die freie Entfaltung seiner Persönlichkeit, soweit er nicht die Rechte anderer verletzt und nicht gegen die verfassungsmäßige Ordnung oder das Sittengesetz verstößt.'

As discussed further below in Chapter 3 the concepts of gender equality cover a spectrum from a concept of formal equality focussing on a narrow ban on direct sex discrimination over other variations of sex discrimination to substantive equality focussing on active elimination of inequalities between the sexes. Article 3 II GG covers aspects of substantive equality while Article 3 III GG only provides for a ban on discrimination. Bleckmann holds that Article 3 III GG is applicable as between private parties to contracts under German law. He thus states:[37]

> Im übrigen Bereich ausserhalb des Arbeitsrechts wird man differenzieren müssen: Der allgemeine Gleichheitssatz findet wohl, weil dem der in Art 2 I verankerte Grundsatz der Vertragsfreihet im Wege steht, im verhältnis zwischen Privaten keine Anwendung. Etwas anderes muss für die in Art 3 III enthaltene Diskriminierungsverbotegelten, die auch auf der internationale Ebene abgesichert sind. Diese Regeln dürften in Anlehnung an die Rechtssprechung des Bundesgerichtshofs zum allgemeinen Persönlichkeitsrecht, die vom BverfG bestätigt worden ist, entweder in Rahmen des § 823 I oder des § 823 II BGB zu Sanktionen führen.

In its Maastricht ruling,[38] the German Constitutional Court (Bundesverfassungsgericht) held that the German Constitution precludes the applicability of secondary Community law which does not respect the basic rights as guaranteed by the German Constitution.

There have only been few collisions between EU labour law and national constitutional provisions. The German Constitution section 12a(4) provides:

> (4) Where, during a state of defence, civilian service requirements in the civilian health system or in the stationary military hospital organization cannot be met on a voluntary basis, women between eighteen and fifty-five years of age can be assigned to such services by or pursuant to a statute. They may in no case render service involving the use of arms.

In *Kreil*,[39] the ECJ held that the Equal treatment Directive[40] precludes the application of national provisions, such as those of German law, which impose

---

[37] Bleckmann, Albert: Staatsrecht II - Die Grundrechte, München 1997 p 737.

[38] Federal Constitutional Court Reporter vol 89, p 155, available at the Internet at http://www.uni-wuerzburg.de/dfr/bv089155.html.

[39] Case C-285/98 *Tanja Kreil* v *Germany* [2000] ECR 0000.

[40] 76/207/EEC.

a general exclusion of women from military posts involving the use of arms and which allow them access only to the medical and military-music services.[41] *Schröder,*[42] *Sievers,*[43] and *Vick*[44] concerned women working part-time who were at some stage during their careers excluded from an occupational retirement pension scheme of the Deutsche Telekom AG and Deutsche Post AG due to the number of hours they worked.

The retroactive effect of the equal pay provision in Article141 EC was limited in *Defrenne (2)*[45] to 1976 and in pension matters the ECJ made a further limitation to 1990 in *Barber*.[46] The German Bundesarbeitsgericht and Bundesverfassungsgericht held that the exclusion of part-time workers was contrary to Article 3(1) GG[47] with effect from its coming into force in 1948.[48]

The employers sought protection under Article141 EC and argued that the objective of equal pay was to prevent distortion of competition and that Article 141 EC which limited the retroactive effect of the equal pay principle in pension matters to 17.5.1990 took precedence over German law, including the German constitution. The ECJ stated fi rst that Article 141 EC aimed to avoid a competitive disadvantage for business enterprise in Member States with more advanced social legislation. Then it recalled that Article 141(2) formulates a social objective for the improvement of the life of workers which extends beyond that of a mere economic union. Also, it stated that in later case law it has held that the right not to be discriminated against on grounds of sex is a fundamental right whose observance the Court has to ensure. The ECJ concluded, as mentioned in Chapter 1:

---

[41] See for a discussion of the *Kreil* case in the light of German constitutional law Müller-Graff, Peter Christian and Friedrich Wenzel Bulst: New Issues in a Sensitive Relationship. Tanja Kreil between secondary EC law and national constitutional law in Europarättslig Tidskrift 2000 p 295.

[42] Case C-50/96, *Schröder* [2000] ECR I-743 paragraph 57.

[43] Joined Cases C270/97 and C271/97,*Sievers* [2000] ECR I-929.

[44] Joined cases C-234/96 og C-235/96, *Vick* [2000] ECR I-799.

[45] Case 43/75 *Defrenne* (No 2) [1976] ECR 455.

[46] Case C-262/88 *Barber* [1990] ECR I-1889.

[47] Which provides: 'Alle Menschen sind vor dem Gesetz gleich'.

[48] See for more detail Besselink, Leonard F M: Commentary to the Schröder case (C-50/96) and others, Common Market Law Review 2001 p 437.

that the economic aim pursued by Article [141 (ex 119)] of the Treaty, namely the elimination of distortions of competition between undertakings established in different Member States, is secondary to the social aim pursued by the same provision, which constitutes the expression of a fundamental human right.

Hence, German law which protected the fundamental right to equality better than Community law was not incompatible with Article 141 EC.

2.6. National equality legislation

At national level, specific Equality Acts prohibiting sex discrimination in various fields of society including some contractual matters other than employment exist in Belgium, Denmark, Finland, Ireland, the Netherlands, Norway and the UK.[49]

In the following, I will present the countries which have adopted specific legislation providing for equal treatment between men and women in contracts for the provision of goods and services in the order in which they have adopted such legislation, ie: UK (1975), Norway (1978), Finland (1986), the Netherlands (1994), Ireland (April 2000), Denmark (May 2000) and Belgium (2003).

2.6.1. United Kingdom[50]

The UK Sex Discrimination Act 1975 contains a prohibition against sex discrimination in the provision of goods, facilities or services.[51] With a few exceptions, it is unlawful to discriminate directly or indirectly on grounds of sex in contracts for the provision of goods, facilities or services to the public, or a section of the public or in the disposal or management of premises.

It is unlawful for any person concerned with the provision (for payment or not) of goods, facilities or services to the public or a section of the public to discriminate against a woman or a man who seeks to obtain or use those goods, facilities or services by refusing or deliberately omitting to provide her (him) with any of them, or by refusing or deliberately omitting to provide her (him)

---

[49] Belgian Loi de 25.2.2003 tendant à lutter contre la discrimination et modifiant la loi du 15 février 1993 créant un Centre pour l'égalité des chances et la lutte contre le racisme, Section 2 of the Danish Equality Act, Section 7 of the Finnish Equality Act, section 5 of the Irish Equal Status Act 2000, section 7 of the Dutch Equality Act, section 3 of the Norwegian Gender Equality Act and Section 29 of Sex Discrimination Act 1975 (as amended).

[50] See generally McCrudden, Christopher: Equality in Law between Men and Women in the European Community, United Kingdom, Luxembourg 1994.

[51] Section 29 of the SDA which is available at www.eoc.org.uk/cseng/legislation/sda.pdf.

with goods, facilities or services of the like quality, in the like manner and on the like terms as are normal in relation to male (female) members of the public.

The following are examples of facilities and services covered by the prohibition against sex discrimination:

access to and use of any place which members of the public or a section of the public are permitted to enter;
accommodation in a hotel, boarding house or other similar establishment;
facilities by way of banking or insurance or for grants, loans, credit or finance;
facilities for education;
facilities for entertainment, recreation or refreshment;
facilities for transport or travel;
the services of any profession or trade, or any local or other public authority.

There is a special derogation in the SDA[52] for insurance and related services. Nothing in the above provisions render unlawful the treatment of a person in relation to an annuity, life assurance policy, accident insurance policy, or similar matter involving the assessment of risk, where the treatment was effected by reference to actuarial or other data from a source on which it was reasonable to rely, and was reasonable having regard to the data and any other relevant factors.

With regard to the use of actuarial factors as a basis for differential treatment of men and women the proposed Directive on equal treatment in contracts for the provision of goods and services[53] clearly goes further than the SDA. This is the most important change adoption of the proposed Directive will require in UK law.

There are also exceptions in the SDA allowing discrimination by non-profit making voluntary bodies restricting their membership to one sex or providing benefits to one sex only in accordance with their main object and allowing discrimination in contracts for the provision of facilities or services to avoid serious embarrassment to users which would be caused by the presence of members of the opposite sex.

The UK SDA contains detailed definitions of various aspects of discrimination, detailed provisions on remedies and establishes a special Equality Body - the Equal Opportunities Commission to oversee the Act,[54] see further below in Chapter 3 and 5.

---

[52] Section 45 SDA.

[53] COM(2003)756.

[54] See www.eoc.org.uk/

Damages cannot be awarded for indirect discrimination in the provision of goods and services under the UK SDA[55] if the respondent proves that the requirement or condition in question was not applied with the *intention* of treating the claimant unfavourably on the ground of his or her sex. The requirement of intention as a precondition for damages makes the UK ban against indirect discrimination in matters of goods and services weak compared to the standard provided for in employment and in the proposed Directive on equal treatment in contracts for the provision of goods and services.

2.6.2. Norway

The Norwegian Gender Equality Act was adopted in 1978. It was intended as a practical instrument for creating de facto gender equality. As the Norwegian Government states at its presentation of the Gender Equality Act on its web site:[56]

> The Nordic philosophy of equality stresses that equal opportunity is not enough. Active efforts are required to promote the status of women.
> The Government assumed that a separate act would play an important role on increasing awareness of the injustices in this area. A separate act would also make it easier to establish a suitable enforcement machinery.

The Norwegian Gender Equality Act[57] applies to all areas of society, except for the internal affairs of religious communities. This includes *inter alia* all areas of contract law. The main rule in the Act is section 3 which provides that direct or indirect differential treatment of women and men is not permitted. The Act contains more detailed provisions on concepts and remedies and sets up a gender specific machinery for the enforcement of the Act. Like its UK counterpart the Norwegian Gender Equality Act[58] provides for a stricter basis of liability for indirect discrimination in matters of employment than in matters of provision of goods and services, see further below in Chapter 3 and 5.

Norway has played a pioneer role in gender mainstreaming[59] in Europe. According to section 1a of the Norwegian Gender Equality Act public authorities shall make active, targeted and systematic efforts to promote gender

---

[55] See further section 66 SDA.

[56] www.likestillingsombudet.no/english/act.html.

[57] An English version is found at www.likestillingsombudet.no/english/act_act.html.

[58] Section 17 of the Act.

[59] http://odin.dep.no/bfd/engelsk/regelverk/rikspolitiske/004041-990030/index-dok000-b-n-a.html.

equality in all sectors of society. Employers shall make active, targeted and systematic efforts to promote gender equality within their enterprise. Employee and employer organizations shall have a corresponding duty to make such efforts in their spheres of activity. Enterprises that are subject to a statutory duty to prepare an annual report shall in the said report give an account of the actual state of affairs as regards gender equality in the enterprise. An account shall also be given of measures that have been implemented and measures that are planned to be implemented in order to promote gender equality and to prevent differential treatment in contravention of this Act.

2.6.3. Finland

Section 6 of the Finnish Constitutions provides for gender equality.[60] The Finnish Act on Equality between Women and Men[61] was passed in 1986.

The Finnish Equality Act contains a general clause which applies to all areas of society which are not explicitly excluded. That includes *inter alia* contract law. The Finnish Equality Act aims at promoting equality between women and men and prohibits direct and indire ct discrimination based on gender. It improves the status of women particularly in working life and gives those discriminated against a right to claim compensation. It obliges the authorities to change such circumstances that prevent the achievement of equality and requires that men and women shall be provided equal opportunities for education and occupational advancement and demands an even distribution of male and female members in state and municipal bodies. The observance of the Act is monitored by the Ombudsman for Equality

---

[60] The Finnish Constitution in English is available at www.oefre.unibe.ch/law/icl/ fi00000_.html Article 6 reads: '(1) Everyone is equal before the law. (2) No one shall, without an acceptable reason, be treated differently from other persons on the ground of sex, age, origin, language, religion, conviction, opinion, health, disability or other reason that concerns his or her person. (3) Children shall be treated equally and as individuals and they shall be allowed to influence matters pertaining to themselves to a degree corresponding to their level of development. (4) Equality of the sexes is promoted in societal activity and working life, especially in the determination of pay and the other terms of employment, as provided in more detail by an Act.'

[61] See section 7 of the Finnish Equality Act, Act no 609 of 8.8.1986 with later amendments, available in English at www.tasa-arvo.fi/www-eng/legislation/ legis2.html.

Section 7[62] which contains a general ban on discrimination received its present form in 1995. Under section 11 an employer who has violated the prohibition on discrimination stipulated in section 8 (which only applies to employers) shall be liable to pay compensation to the affected person. The Finnish Act does not provide for any specific remedy for violation of the general ban on discrimination in section 7 of the Act which applies to discrimination in contracts for the provision of goods and services, see further below in Chapter 5.

2.6.4. The Netherlands

Article 1 of the Dutch Constitution prohibits discrimination.[63] The 1994 Dutch Equality Act[64] elaborates on this norm. It prohibits discrimination in specific fields (employment, education and the provision of goods and services) on a limited number of grounds (religion, belief, political orientation, race, sex, nationality, sexual preference, marital status, working hours or temporary contract). The Equal Treatment Commission was set up to promote and monitor compliance with this Act, together with other specific non-discrimination and equal treatment legislation in the Netherlands.

Section 7 of the 1994 Dutch Equality Act provides that it shall be unlawful to discriminate in offering goods or services and in concluding, implementing or terminating agreements on the subject in the course of carrying on a business or exercising a profession; by the public service; by institutions which are active in the field of housing, social services, health care, cultural affairs or education or by private persons not engaged in carrying on a business or exercising a profession, in so far as the offer is made publicly.

---

[62] Section 7 of the Finnish Equality Act reads: Prohibition of discrimination. Direct or indirect discrimination on the basis of sex is prohibited. For the purposes of this Act, discrimination on the basis of sex means: (1) treating men and women differently on the basis of sex; (2) treating women differently for reasons of pregnancy or childbirth; or (3) treating men and women differently on the basis of parenthood, family responsibilities or for some other reason related to sex. Discrimination is also involved in any procedure whereby people are de facto assigned a different status in relation to each other for the reasons mentioned in paragraph 2.

[63] The Dutch constitution is available in English at www.oefre.unibe.ch/law /icl/nl00000_.html. Article 1 reads: 'All persons in the Netherlands shall be treated equally in equal circumstances. Discrimination on the grounds of religion, belief, political opinion, race, or sex or on any other grounds whatsoever shall not be permitted.'

[64] Algemene wet gelijke behandeling, AWGB. A translation into English is available at the Commissie Gelijke Behandeling's homepage www.cgb.nl/english/asp/awgb.asp.

The Dutch Equality Act defines the concepts of direct and indirect discrimination see further Chapter 3. It allows for positive action.[65] There are no gender mainstreaming provisions in the Act but the Netherlands does pursue a policy of gender mainstreaming.[66]

Contractual provisions which conflict with the Act are null and void.[67] Apart from that the Act does not contain provisions on remedies outside of the employment field.

The Dutch Equality Act establishes an Equal Treatment Commission Commissie Gelijke Behandeling) with powers to investigate alleged violations of the Act and bring legal proceedings, see further Chapter 5.

2.6.5. Ireland

Under Article 40 of the Irish Constitution[68] all citizens shall, as human persons, be held equal before the law.

Ireland adopted an Equal Status Act[69] in 2000 which prohibits discrimination on a number of grounds including gender. Section 5 of the Act provides that a person shall not discriminate in disposing of goods to the public generally or a section of the public or in providing a service, whether the disposal or provision is for consideration or otherwise and whether the service provided can be availed of only by a section of the public. Under section 6 of the Act a person shall not discriminate in

(a) disposing of any estate or interest in premises,

(b) terminating any tenancy or other interest in premises, or

(c) providing accommodation or any services or amenities related to accommodation or ceasing to provide accommodation or any such services or amenities.

The Act allows for positive action.[70] It contains elaborate definitions of key concepts and enforcement provisions, see further in Chapter 3 and 5.

---

[65] See section 2(3) of the Act.

[66] See further at the Ministry of Employment and Social Aggairs' homepage at internationalezaken.szw.nl/index.cfm?fuseaction=dsp_rubriek&rubriek_id=13021&lijstm=0,310_6060.

[67] See section 9 of the Act.

[68] Available at www.oefre.unibe.ch/law/icl/ei00000_.html.

[69] www.odei.ie/Web-Images/EqualStatusAct2000.pdf.

[70] In section Section 14(b)(i) of the Act.

2.6.6. Denmark

The Danish Constitution contains no provision on gender equality. In 2000, an Act on Equality between Women and Men was adopted.[71] The Act lays down a general prohibition against discrimination on grounds of sex in all fields of society and introduces a private law remedy of compensation for both economic and non-economic loss available to all aggrieved individuals. In addition the Act establishes a machinery for enforcement both of the general Act on Equality and the more specialized acts on equal pay, equal treatment in working life and equal treatment in matters of occupational pension schemes.

Section 1 of the Act states that its purpose is to promote equality between women and men, including equal integration, equal influence and equal opportunities in all functions in society based on the equal value of women and men. Furthermore it is the purpose of the Act to counteract direct and indirect discrimination on grounds of sex and to discourage sexual harassment. Section 2[72] of the Act prohibits sex discrimination.

The Act on Equality defines direct and indirect sex discrimination including sexual harassment and establishes an Equality Complaints Board[73] to hear complaints over alleged sex discrimination in violation of the Equality Act 2000, the Equal Pay Act, the Equal Treatment Act and the Act on equality in respect of occupational pension schemes, see further below in Chapter 3 and 5.

2.6.7. Belgium

Article 10 and 11 of the Belgian Constitution[74] provides that Belgians are equal before the law and that enjoyment of the rights and freedoms recognized for Belgians should be ensured without discrimination.

In Belgium a 'Loi tendant à lutter contre la discrimination et modifiant la loi du 15 février 1993 créant un Centre pour l'égalité des changes et la lutte contre le racisme' was adopted in February 2003.[75] The Act contains no provisions on

---

[71] The Danish Equality Act is available in English at http://ligestillinguk.itide.dk/Default.asp?Id=194.

[72] The provision reads: 'Women and men shall receive equal treatment by employers, authorities or organisations within the public administration and in connection with business and general activities. Any person whose rights under the first sentence are violated may be awarded compensation.'

[73] See further www.ligenaevn.dk.

[74] Available in English at www.oefre.unibe.ch/law/icl/be00000_.html.

[75] Loi de 25.2.2003. Loi tendant à lutter contre la discrimination et modifiant la loi du 15 février 1993 créant un Centre pour l'égalité des changes et la lutte contre le racisme, published in Moniteur Belge 17.3.2003. Moniteur Belge is available online at

gender-mainstreaming but allows positive action.[76] It defines direct and indirect sex discrimination and sexual harassment but not other harassment on grounds of sex. It prohibits incitement to discriminate and victimisation. Article 2(4) of the Act provides:

> Toute discrimination directe ou indirecte est interdite, lorsqu'elle porte sur la fourniture ou la mise à la disposition du public de biens et de services.

The Belgian Equality Act provides for both criminal (typically a fine) and civil sanctions for violation of the Act, see further below in Chapter 5. Special bodies on gender equality were established by separate laws.[77]

2.7. Standard elements in gender equality legislation

As appears from the above existing and proposed gender equality legislation contains a number of standard elements. The basic concepts (gender mainstreaming, positive action, sex discrimination (direct and indirect, harassment and sexual harassment), incitement to discriminate and victimisation are discussed in more detail below in Chapter 3, the scope of the ban on discrimination in Chapter 4 and remedies, enforcement, burden of proof and special equality bodies in Chapter 5.

2.7.1. Gender mainstreaming
Gender mainstreaming provisions applying to the field of contract law (outside of employment) are found in the EC-Treaty and the Nordic countries and Germany. Such provisions mainly put obligations on public authorities (including national courts) and have only limited horizontal effect between the parties to contracts.

2.7.2. Positive action
Positive action is allowed by EU law in the sense that it is up to the Member States to decide whether they will allow or prohibit such measures. Under UK law positive action is as the main rule prohibited. Apart from the UK SDA all the national equality Acts allow for some measures of positive action.

---

www.just.fgov.be/index_fr.htm.

[76] See Article 4 of the Act.

[77] See Loi (16.12.2002) portant création de l'Institutpour l'égalité des femmes et des hommes (homepage at http://meta.fgov.be/pa/paa/framesetfrcg00.htm) and Arrêté royal (4.4.2003) portant réorganisation du Conseil de l'égalité des chances entre hommes et femmes.

2.7.3. Definitions of sex discrimination (direct and indirect sex discrimination, harassment and sexual harassment, incitement to discriminate and victimisation)

The most elaborate definition of sex discrimination, comprising direct and indirect sex discrimination, harassment and sexual harassment, incitement to discriminate and victimisation is found in the proposed Directive on equal treatment in the provision of goods and services. All existing national gender-specific laws in this area contain definitions of aspects of sex discrimination as defined by the proposed Directive but also lack some aspects of the EU concept of sex discrimination.

2.7.4. Fairly broad prohibition of sex discrimination outside of employment

The national gender-specific legislation prohibiting sex discrimination outside of employment typically covers more than the provision of goods and services including for example advertising and education.

Insurance based on gender related actuarial factors is explicitly exempted in the UK SDA. In the other countries it is less clear whether and to what extent sex discrimination by reference to actuarial factors is lawful under current legislation but in practice such discrimination occurs.

2.7.5. Remedies

The Belgian Gender Equality Act provides for both criminal (a fine) and civil sanctions but the general pattern is that the focus is on civil law remedies, typically monetary compensation. The Finnish Gender Equality Act does not provide for any specific remedy in matters outside of employment. The UK and Norwegian legislation provides for a more lenient basis of liability with regard to sex discrimination in contracts for the provision of goods and services as compared with the liability standard applying in employment matters.

Under EU law it is for the Member States to choose the remedies but EU law lays down some framework conditions through the general principles of EU law and specific provisions in directives. The proposed Directive on equal treatment in the provision of goods and services contains such additional requirements to ensure the effectiveness of the proposed ban on sex discrimination.

2.7.6. Special Equality bodies

All EU countries have set up some kind of special equality machinery. In countries with specific gender equality legislation such bodies also have some powers to take part in legal enforcement. The proposed Directive lays down more precise provisions in this regard.

2.7.7. Burden of proof

It is a standard provision in EU discrimination law to shift the burden of proof from the complainant to the respondent once the plaintiff has established facts before a court or other body from which it may be presumed that discrimination has taken place. The proposed Directive on equal treatment in the provision of goods and services continues this tradition which by and large has no counterpart at national level, see further below in Chapter 5.

2.8. What difference will adoption of the proposed Directive make?

In respect of gender mainstreaming the proposed Directive will make no difference.

In respect of sex discrimination, most EU citizens live in countries where there are no legislation on this issue in matters outside of employment. Compared to existing national gender equality legislation the proposed Directive lays down more far-reaching definitions of the basic concepts and more detailed and elaborate provisions on remedies and enforcement including a duty to establish specific equality bodies with powers to assist in legal enforcement and to shift the burden of proof in order to make the substantive provisions prohibiting sex discrimination effective.

In most respects (advertising, education, taxation, etc) the scope of the proposed Directive is narrower than that of many national equality Acts but it is broader in respect of actuarial factors in insurance and financial services which is particularly important from a practical and economic point of view.

The proposed Directive contains no explicit transparency requirements. Such requirements are, however, to some extent included in the justification test which forms part of the concept of indirect discrimination, see further below in Chapter 3. Lack of transparency has consequences for the burden of proof, see below in Chapter 5.

3. Gender Equality as a Fundamental Right and General Principle of EU Law

3.1. Sources of fundamental rights in Community law

EU respects[78] fundamental rights, as guaranteed by the ECHR and as they result from the constitutional traditions common to the Member States, as general principles of Community law. In the preamble to the EU Charter of Fundamental

---

[78] According to Article 6 EU.

Rights,[79] which is incorporated in the draft Constitutional Treaty for the EU, it is stated that the Charter reaffirms the fundamental rights as they result, in particular, from the constitutional traditions and international obligations common to the Member States, the Treaty on European Union, the Community Treaties, the ECHR, the Social Charters adopted by the Union and by the Council of Europe and the case law of the ECJ and of the ECtHR.

The first recital in the Preamble to the proposed Directive on equal treatment in the provision of goods and services[80] refers to Article 6(2) EU and the second recital states that the right to equality before the law and protection against discrimination for all persons constitutes a universal right recognised in a number of international treaties to which all EU countries are signatories.

3.1.1. Constitutional traditions and international obligations common to the Member States

As set out above there are gender equality provisions in many national constitutions but their consequences for contract law are limited.

The UN Convention on the Elimination of All Forms of Discrimination against Women (CEDAW) was adopted in 1979. CEDAW which entered into force 3 September 1981, was, as of 10 December 2003, ratified by 175 countries, ie more than 90% of UN member states, including all EU countries.[81]

So far, CEDAW has only played a limited role in Community law and an even more limited role in European contract law. There is however, reference to it in the preambles to all the discrimination directives adopted or proposed since 2000 by DG Employment, ie the directive on race,[82] the framework directive (which prohibits discrimination on grounds of religion, age, handicap and sexual orientation in employment),[83] the directive on equal treatment for men and women in employment and occupation[84] and the pending proposal for a Directive on equal treatment of men and women in the provision of goods and services.[85]

---

[79] See europa.eu.int/comm/justice_home/unit/charte/en/rights.html.

[80] COM(2003)756.

[81] See for details www.un.org/womenwatch/daw/cedaw/states.htm.

[82] 2000/43/EC.

[83] 2000/78/EC.

[84] 2002/73/EC.

[85] Recital 2 in COM(2003)756.

The draft proposal for a Directive on Services, presented in 2004 by DG Markt, which contains a prohibition against discrimination on grounds of nationality and residence[86] does not refer to CEDAW.

The most important contract law provisions in CEDAW are found in Article 13(b) which provides that States Parties shall take all appropriate measures to eliminate discrimination against women in the right to bank loans, mortgages and other forms of financial credit and in Article 15 which requires States Parties to accord to women, in civil matters, a legal capacity identical to that of men and the same opportunities to exercise that capacity. In particular, they shall give women equal rights to conclude contracts. States Parties agree that all contracts and all other private instruments of any kind with a legal effect which is directed at restricting the legal capacity of women shall be deemed null and void.

The Preamble to the Social Charter adopted by the Council of Europe in 1961 states that enjoyment of social rights should be secured without discrimination on grounds of sex and a number of other criteria.

In contrast, the prohibition of sex discrimination in Article 14 ECHR does not confer an autonomous substantive right. It only applies in conjunction with another Article of the ECHR or its Protocols.[87] EU accession to the ECHR will therefore not add much to the existing ban on sex discrimination. On 26 June 2000 the Committee of Ministers adopted a new Protocol No 12 to the ECHR. Article 1 of this convention provides for a general prohibition against discrimination[88] but the Protocol has not entered into force.[89]

3.1.2. Case law of the ECJ
Historically, the ECJ was the first to discover gender equality as a fundamental right and a general principle of Community law.

---

[86] available at europa.eu.int/comm/internal_market/en/services/services/docs/2004-proposal_en.pdf. It is provisional and subject to further linguistic revisions.

[87] Protocol 12 to the ECHR provides for a free-standing prohibition of sex discrimination. Denmark, France, Spain, Sweden and the UK as well as a number of the candidate countries are not signatories to Protocol 12.

[88] Article 1 reads: General prohibition of discrimination. 1.The enjoyment of any right set forth in law shall be secured without discrimination on any ground such as sex, race, colour, language, religion, political or other opinion, national or social origin, associated with a national minority, property, birth or other status

[89] Only 5 countries (no EU countries) have ratified it. It requires 10 ratification to come into force, see further http://conventions.coe.int/Treaty/Commun/Cherche-Sig.asp?NT=177&CM=8&DF=03/03/04&CL=ENG.

In 1972, in *Sabbatini*,[90] the Court annulled a decision, which was in accordance with the Parliament's Staff Regulation, to withdraw a female staff members' expatriation allowance because she married and did not become 'head of household'. The ECJ held that the decision to withdraw the woman's allowance was sex discriminatory and therefore devoid of any legal basis. It was consequently annulled under Article 230 EC. In *Sabbatini*, the Court thus held that the principle of equal treatment limits the power of EU institutions.

The ECJ has, since the ruling in *Defrenne* (3) in 1978, described equality between men and women as a fundamental right and a general principle of law.[91] *Defrenne* (3) concerned a conflict between a female employee and her private sector employer whose contracts with female employees contained a clause bringing the contract to an end when the woman reached the age of 40. Contracts with male employees did not contain a similar clause. The facts underlying the case happened before the adoption of the Equal Treatment Directive[92] at a time where the only explicitly binding Community provision on gender equality was the equal pay provision in Article 141 EC [then Article 119]. The referring Belgian court put a question to the ECJ as to the possible existence of a general principle of Community law, the aim of which is to eliminate discrimination between men and women workers as regards conditions of employment and working conditions other than remuneration in the strict sense. In its reply to that question the ECJ held:

26. The Court has repeatedly stated that respect for fundamental personal human rights is one of the general principles of Community law, the observance of which it has a duty to ensure.
27. There can be no doubt that the elimination of discrimination based on sex forms part of those fundamental rights.

As appears, the ECJ in its reply did not limit itself to the employment field but stated its holding by means of a broad wording which would apply equally to sex discriminatory contractual terms outside of the labour market.

The ECJ invoked the principle of effective judicial protection as a fundamental principle of EU law in *Johnston*.[93] The Court stated regarding Article 6 of the Equal Treatment Directive (emphasis added):

---

[90] Case 20-71, *Luisa Sabbatini* v *European Parliament* [1972] ECR 345.

[91] Case 149/77 *Defrenne* v *Sabena* (No 3) [1978] ECR 1365.

[92] 76/207/EEC. Since the implementation of that directive there is no doubt that different age limits for male and female staff in employment contracts are unlawful.

[93] Case 222/84, *Johnston* [1986] ECR 1651.

The requirement of judicial control stipulated by that article reflects a general principle of law which underlies the constitutional traditions common to the Member States. That principle is also laid down in articles 6 and 13 of the European Convention for the Protection of Human Rights and Fundamental Freedoms of 4 November 1950. (...) By virtue of Article 6 of Directive no 76/207, interpreted in the light of the general principle stated above, *all persons have the right to obtain an effective remedy in a competent court against measures which they consider to be contrary to the principle of equal treatment for men and women* laid down in the directive.

There must thus be a competent court in accordance with the rules laid down in Articles 6 and 13 ECHR which have been developed further in Article II-47 of the draft Constitutional Treaty, see below in Chapter 5.

3.2. Applicability of the general EU principle of equal treatment

3.2.1. Binding in EU law

In *Rinke*[94] the question was put to the ECJ as to whether the prohibition of indirect discrimination on grounds of sex constitutes a basic unwritten right under Community law that overrides any conflicting rule in secondary Community legislation. The case was about two freedom of establishment directives[95] for doctors and the problem was whether a requirement laid down in the directives to the effect that certain components of the specific training in general medical practice must be undertaken full-time constitutes indirect sex discrimination. The ECJ stated in the operative part of the judgment (which is a full court decision) in general terms:

Compliance with the prohibition of indirect discrimination on grounds of sex is a condition governing the legality of all measures adopted by the Community institutions.

The ECJ thus found that the EU legislator and any other Community institution when adopting secondary EU law and any other measure that can be taken under EU law must respect the fundamental principle of elimination of indirect discrimination on grounds of sex. With regard to the individual directives at issue in *Rinke* the ECJ held that they were not in violation of that principle.

It follows from the above that all EU contract law measures in order to be valid must respect the general principle of gender equality.

---

[94] Case C-25/02, *Rinke* [2003] ECR I-0000 (nyr).

[95] 86/457/EEC and 93/16/EEC.

3.2.2. No indirect horizontal effect when the principle of equal treatment stands alone

As mentioned above, the ECJ in *Defrenne* (3) considered equality between men and women a fundamental right and a general principle of law. The ECJ did, however, add that at the time of the events of the case the Community had not assumed any responsibility for supervising and guaranteeing the observance of the principle of equality between men and women in working conditions other than remuneration. The ECJ stated:[96]

> It follows that the situation before the Belgian courts is governed by the provisions and principles of internal and international law in force in Belgium.

The ECJ thus did not consider the Community principle of elimination of discrimination based on sex applicable in national law where the application of Community law was not involved. The fundamental principles may be relied upon by individuals and must be taken into account by the national courts, not in any circumstances, but only in cases which display some connection with the legal order of the Community.

Applied on contract law that means that all those general contract law issues - eg concerning formation and validity - which are not (yet) governed by EU law cannot be subjected to criticism for not complying with the general Community law principle of gender equality. When (and if) the proposal for a Directive on equal treatment in the provision of goods and services is adopted practically all aspects of contract law will come under EU law control with regard to compliance with the general principle of gender equality.

3.2.3. Indirect horizontal effect in areas involving EU law, eg EU consumer contract law

Under the *acquis communautaire* Member States are bound by the fundamental rights including the fundamental right of gender equality when they act within the field of Community law as for example the freedom to provide services in Article 49 EC.[97]

Applied on contract law this means that the principle of equal treatment between men and women must be observed in national law within the scope of

---

[96] Case 149/77 *Defrenne* v *Sabena* (No 3) [1978] ECR 1365 paragraph 32.

[97] See case Case 5/88, *Wachauf* [1989] ECR 2609, C-260/89, *ERT* [1991] ECR I-2925 and case C-60/00, *Carpenter* [2002] ECR I-6279.

all the existing contract law directives, for example on unfair terms in consumer contracts[98] or door-step selling.[99]

Gender-neutral EU contract law provisions thus drag the principle of equal treatment of men and women into (parts of) national contract law because general principles of EU law must be observed in national law in all areas where the application of Community law is involved and the principle of gender equality is one of the general principles of EU law.

3.2.4. Direct horizontal effect of Article II-21 in the Constitutional Treaty

As mentioned Article II-21(1) provides for a broad ban on discrimination on a number of grounds including sex.[100] The question discussed in the following is whether this provision when (and if) the draft Constitutional Treaty is adopted will acquire direct horizontal effect as binding upon private individuals in areas involving Community law also when there is nothing in national law it can be interpreted into for example because the proposed Directive on equal treatment, after being adopted, is not correctly implemented.

It is settled case law that directives are not directly binding against private individuals. In *Dori*,[101] the ECJ thus held that in the absence of measures transposing the directive concerning protection of the consumer in respect of contracts negotiated away from business premises[102] within the prescribed time-limit, consumers cannot derive from the directive itself a right of cancellation as against traders with whom they have concluded a contract or enforce such a right in a national court.

As regards Treaty provisions the rule is different. Generally a Treaty provision has direct, horizontal effect if it is sufficiently clear and precise. The ECJ has developed this rule with equal pay between men and women as the starting point. Already in 1976, the ECJ held that Article 141 EC on equal pay, has direct horizontal effect as binding upon private individuals.[103]

---

[98] Directive 93/13/EEC of 5 April 1993 on unfair terms in consumer contracts.

[99] 85/577/EEC.

[100] Article II-21(1) reads: Any discrimination based on any ground such as sex, race, colour, ethnic or social origin, genetic features, language, religion or belief, political or any other opinion, membership of a national minority, property, birth, disability, age or sexual orientation shall be prohibited.

[101] Case C-91/92, *Paola Faccini Dori* [1994] ECR I-3325.

[102] 85/577/EEC.

[103] Case 43/75, *Defrenne* (No 2) [1976] ECR 455.

In my view the ban on sex discrimination in Article II-21 of the draft Constitutional Treaty is as clear and precise as for example Article 141 EC and therefore must be also directly applicable in national law involving EU law against private businesses. In the *Dori* case the aggrieved consumer was approached by a seller at Milan Railway Station who sold her an English language correspondence course. The contract was concluded away from the seller's business premises but Italy had not implemented the directive on that problem. If, in addition, a seller in such a situation charges higher prices for women than men, the buyer will, once the Constitutional Treaty has come into force, be able to rely directly on Article II-21 against the seller in the same way as an employee can rely on Article 141 EC against a private employer.

In *Coloroll*,[104] the ECJ held that a worker can rely directly on Article 141 EC not only against an employer but also against the trustees of a pension scheme in respect of employment related pension contracts. Sex discrimination in pension contracts outside of employment is a very practical and controversial issue, see further below in Chapter 4. It may therefore become a practical area for direct effect of the forthcoming Article II-21 in the Constitutional Treaty.

Article II-21 will only become directly applicable in areas governed by EU law. In *Dory*,[105] the ECJ held that Community law does not govern the Member States' choices of military organisation, including whether or not to make military service compulsory, and if so whether it should be only for men and not for women. Article II-21 will not be applicable in such areas.[106]

The provision in Article II-23[107] of the draft Constitutional Treaty is less precise than Article II-21 and can probably not become directly applicable.

3.2.5. Rights and principles
Article 52 of the Charter of fundamental rights on 'Scope and interpretation of rights and principles' codifies the distinction between rights and principles.[108] Rights shall be respected, whereas principles shall be observed. Principles may

---

[104] Case C-200/91 *Coloroll* v *James Russell and others* [1994] ECR I-4389.

[105] Case C-186/01, *Alexander Dory* [2003] ECR I-2479.

[106] See also Article 51(2) of the Charter of Fundamental Rights which provides that the Charter does not extend the field of application of EU law.

[107] Article II-23 provides: Equality between men and women must be ensured in all areas, including employment, work and pay. The principle of equality shall not prevent the maintenance or adoption of measures providing for specific advantages in favour of the under-represented sex.

[108] It has been discussed in legal theory for a number of years, see for example Dworkin, Ronald: Taking Rights Seriously, London 1977.

be implemented through legislative or executive acts. According to the explanatory remarks to the Charter, they become significant for the Courts only when such acts are interpreted or reviewed. They do not give rise to direct claims for positive action by the Union's institutions or Member States authorities.

In some cases, an Article of the Charter may contain both elements of a right and of a principle. The explanatory remarks to Article 52 mentions Article 23 as an example of such a provision which is a mixture of a right and a principle.

4. The Gender Dimension in Gender-neutral Sources of Contract Law

A number of formally gender neutral contract rules can (probably) be invoked with regard to gender equality in contractual transactions.

4.1. National contract law

In comparison to EU contract law, national contract law is an old and settled kind of law where the expert legal culture is well developed and where the main principles were established some hundred years ago. In contract law the gender dimension is, as mentioned in Chapter 1, much more visible at the surface level of the law[109] than in the underlying sub-surface layers of the legal culture and the deep structure of law. In mainstream scholarly writing on national contract law the gender dimension is by and large not explicitly integrated.

4.2. EU contract law Acquis

As the DG Markt states at its contract law web site[110]

> EU instruments which have an impact on contract law in the member states (often referred to as the EU's contract law acquis) can be found in many areas. A large number of these fall within the Commission's Internal Market policy. A similarly large number are relating to the Health and Consumer Affairs. Most of these instruments harmonise specific aspects of contract law in the member states. However, free circulation of goods and services can also be facilitated by allowing parties to choose which (national) law should govern their contract. Information about the various instruments which are relevant in this area can be found on the applicable law section of the Justice and Home Affairs website.

---

[109] See on the levels of law Tuori, Kaarlo: Critical Legal Positivism, Aldershot 2002 Chapter 6.

[110] europa.eu.int/comm/internal_market/contractlaw/links_en.htm.

In addition, labour law and discrimination law related to contracts (also outside of employment) are anchored in DG Employment. In other matters than employment and occupation a considerable part of the existing EC directives on contract law deal with consumer law. The most important directives on consumer protection are the directive on door-step selling,[111] the consumer credit directive,[112] the directives on distance contracts,[113] the directive on unfair terms in consumer contracts[114] and the directive on the sale of consumer goods.[115] Generally the consumer protection directives deal with commercial communications, information to be provided before the conclusion of the contract and conclusion of the contract and contractual obligations. Commercial communications are dealt with in several directives.

The favoured method in EU consumer law directives is to improve market transparency while leaving well-informed consumers with a very wide scope of freedom to make consumer choices.[116]

Consumer contracts are probably more than business contracts gender related since many consumers are women who often live under other social conditions than men. This is for example true with regard to surety contracts, see further below in Chapter 4. A consumer surety is often a woman, either a wife who stands surety for her husband or an elderly mother who stands surety for her son. A typical function of a consumer surety contract is to transfer money from women to men.

EU contract law is a young and dynamic set of law. At the present stage of development it is still fragmentary and incoherent - a fact that has been widely commented upon both at national and EU level. Scandinavian authors with a background in consumer law have expressed concern over the impact of EU law because of the challenge to the traditional flexibility of the Nordic model it constitutes. In a discussion of the then proposal for the Directive on unfair

---

[111] 85/577/EEC.

[112] 87/102/EEC with later amendments.

[113] 97/7/EC on the protection of consumers in respect of distance contracts and 2002/65/EC concerning the distance marketing of consumer financial services.

[114] Directive 93/13/EEC of 5 April 1993 on unfair terms in consumer contracts.

[115] Directive 1999/44/EC on certain aspects of the sale of consumer goods and associated guarantees.

[116] See Grundmann, Stefan: Information, Party Autonomy and Economic Agents in European Contract Law in Common Market Law Review 2002 p 269.

terms in consumer contracts[117] Wilhelmsson argued that much of the critique of the proposal was connected with its effects on the contract models or paradigms. The negative impact of the Directive lies, according to him, in the fact that it may weaken tendencies towards the acceptance of new contract models in Nordic law. In general these tendencies imply a shift from a formal or content-neutral contract model, within which the events at the time of the conclusion of the contract are decisive for the content of the contractual obligation, towards a more material or content-oriented model where the substantive fairness of the outcome of a contract is of primary relevance when deciding whether a contractual obligation is binding. The term social contract law has been used to describe this trend in the development of Nordic law.[118]

4.3. The Action Plan on European Contract Law 2003

4.3.1. Background

The official actors in EU law (EU Council, EU Commission and the European Parliament) as well as representatives of the Member States' governments have all engaged in the debate as to whether it is desirable to promote further Europeanization of private law, including core areas of contract law, and, if so, with what legal means that could and should be done.

In broad terms, the European Parliament favours a uniform codification of (parts of) private law, while the EU Council and EU Commission are more cautious. In 1989 and 1994 the Europea n Parliament passed Resolutions requesting a start to be made on the necessary preparatory work on drawing up a European Code of Private Law. In the 1989 Resolution it is stated that:[119]

'unification can be carried out in branches of private law which are highly important for the development of a Single Market, such as contract law....'

---

[117]   93/13/EEC.

[118]   Wilhelmsson, Thomas: The Proposal for an Unfair Contracts Directive - a Nordic Perspective, European Consumer Law Journal 1992 p 77. See also Wilhelmsson, Thomas: European Contract Law Harmonization: Aims and Tools, Tulane Journal of International & Comparative Law 1993 and Wilhelmsson, Thomas: Critical Studies in Private Law, Deventer 1992 which is a revised English translation of a Finnish work entitled Social kontraktsrätt.

[119]   See OJ 1989 C 158/400 and OJ 1994 C 205/ 518.

When the Commission proposed[120] the Consumer Sales Directive[121] it stated that the proposal took the European Parliament's endeavours to encourage approximation of the private law of the Member States into account and included a reference to the above Parliament resolutions.

Art 61 EC (as amended by the Amsterdam Treaty) provides that the Council in order to establish progressively an area of freedom, security and justice, shall adopt measures in the field of judicial cooperation in civil matters as provided for in Article 65. The Conclusions of the European Council meeting in Tampere on 15 and 16 October 1999 stated under the heading[122] 'Greater convergence in civil law' that the European Council invited the Council and the Commission to prepare new procedural legislation in cross-border cases, in particular on those elements which are instrumental to smooth judicial co-operation and to enhanced access to law, e.g. provisional measures, taking of evidence, orders for money payment and time limits. As regards substantive law, an overall study is requested on the need to approximate Member States' legislation in civil matters in order to eliminate obstacles to the good functioning of civil proceedings.

In March 2000, the European Commission presented a communication on a Scoreboard to review progress on the creation of an area of 'Freedom, security and justice" in the European Union.[123]

In July 2001, the Commission submitted a Communication on European Contract Law.[124] The Commission invited Member States governments and, via its contract law website on the internet,[125] all other interested persons or organisations to respond to the Communication. The replies received are made available at this website. In its 2001 communication on European contract law,[126] the European Commission presented four options for discussion:

---

[120] COM(95)520 p 4.

[121] 99/44/EC.

[122] The Resolution is available at the Europa server at europa.eu.int/council/off/conclu/dec99/dec99_en.htm.

[123] COM(2000)167.

[124] COM(2001)398.

[125] europa.eu.int/comm/consumers/cons_int/safe_shop/ fair_bus_pract/cont_law/index_en.htm.

[126] COM(2001)398.

1) leave the solution of any identified problems to the market,
2) promote the development of non-binding common contract law principles, that can be used in standard contracts or in the drafting of national rules, etc
3) review and improve (simplify and clarify) existing Community legislation in the area of contract law to make it more coherent or to adapt it to cover situations not foreseen at the time of adoption,
4) adopt a new instrument at EU level

4.3.2. Options in the 2003 Action Plan on European contract law
In February 2003, the Commission issued a communication[127] where it confirmed that there is no need to abandon the current sector-specific approach. The Action Plan suggests a mix of non-regulatory and regulatory measures.. In addition to appropriate sector-specific interventions, this includes measures :

- to increase the coherence of the EC acquis in the area of contract law,
- to promote the elaboration of EU-wide general contract terms, and
- to examine further whether problems in the European contract law area may require non sector-specific solutions such as an optional instrument.

The Commission again invited interested persons or organisations to respond to the Communication. The replies received are available at its contract law website. The present author submitted a contribution on the gender aspect,[128] but the other responses didn't address this issue.

Compared with the 2001 communication the option of leaving it to the market to solve any problems is left out. Apart from that the options discussed in the 2003 action plan are in broad terms the same as those set out in the 2003 communication.

4.3.3. Academic discussion
In academic circles there has been a vivid debate for or against a European Civil Code[129] or other kinds of Europeanisation of private law for a number of years. Much of the debate on European contract law has been conducted by academics who by and large have ignored the gender dimension.

---

[127] COM(2003)68. 'A More Coherent European Contract Law - an Action Plan'.

[128] See europa.eu.int/comm/consumers/cons_int/safe_shop/fair_bus_pract/cont_law/ stake holders/5-37.pdf.

[129] See generally on this possibility Hartkamp, A S, M W Hesselink, E H Hondius, C Joustra and E du Perron (eds), Towards a European Civil Code, Kluwer Law International 1998.

Much of the debate on European contract law has been conducted by academics who by and large have ignored the gender dimension.

The *UNIDROIT Principles* of International Commercial Contracts, published in June 1994, are a sort of international restatement of contract law.[130] The so-called Lando-Commission on European Contract Law has been drafting the *Principles of European Contract Law* since 1980.[131] These, like the UNIDROIT Principles, constitute a restatement of principles for the general part of contract law in Europe. The gender-dimension is absent from the Principles of European Contract Law as described by the Lando-Commission. They do not address the question as to whether the principle of gender equality is a general principle of European contract law. Lando[132] states in a response to the EU Commission's Action Plan on European contract Law 2003[133] that the main purpose of the Principles of European Contract Law is to serve as a first draft of a part of a European Civil Code.

The European Principles of Contract Law are, however, not only gender-blind, but also EU blind. They do not take notice of Community law, neither of the case law of the ECJ nor of the legislative developments in the field of contracts nor of the general principles of Community law which as set out above includes the principle of equal treatment between men and women. The approach taken by the European Principles is the traditional comparative method which is confined to legal systems existing at the national level. The Lando-Commission analyses the *national acquis* in European contract law but not the *acquis communautaire*. As set out above in Chapter 1, section 4 comparative law is in the process of taking over a new dimension due to the interaction of EU law and national law. The Lando-Commission's lack of interest in Community law will probably make

---

[130] J. Lookofsky, 'The Limits of Commercial Contract Freedom: Under the UNI-DROIT 'Restatement' and Danish Law' in American Journal of Comparative Law 1998 p 485.

[131] See further www.cbs.dk/departments/law/staff/ol/commission_on_ecl/index.html. Lando, Ole and Hugh Beale (eds): Principles of European Contract Law. Parts I and II, The Hague, London, Boston, Kluwer Law International 2000 and Lando, Ole, Eric Clive, Andre Prum and Reinhard Zimmerman: Principles of European Contract Law. Part III, The Hague, London, Boston, Aspen Publishers 2003..

[132] europa.eu.int/comm/consumers/cons_int/safe_shop/fair_bus_pract/cont_law/sta keholders/5-31.pdf.

[133] COM(2003) 68.

it less attractive for EU actors to build on the Principles of European Contract Law in the furhter development of EU contract law.[134]

The Study Group on a European Civil Code[135] commenced its work in the middle of 1999. The Group is addressing the law governing certain particular types of contract (sales, services, credit agreements and credit securities, contracts of insurance, and long-term commercial contracts: agency, distribution and franchise contracts), the law of non contractual obligations (tort law, the law of unjustified enrichments and the law on negotiorum gestio) and those parts of the law of movable property which are particularly relevant to the functioning of the internal market (credit securities in movables, transfer of ownership in movables and, prospectively, the law of trusts).

The Common Core Project[136] looks into hypothetical cases and solve them under the law of the several European countries. So far, it has not addressed the question as to whether there is a common core in European contract law in matters of gender equality law.

As a reaction on activities of EU institutions in the field of European contract law, the Acquis Project[137] targets a systematic arrangement of existing Community law which will help to elucidate the common structures of the emerging Community private law. In order to achieve this, the Acquis Group primarily concentrates upon the existing EC private law which can be discovered within the *acquis communautaire*.

4.4. The proposed equality Directive and the Action Plan on contract law compared

In the following I will highlight the main differences and similarities between the proposed equality Directive, and the Action Plan on contract law.

4.4.1. Main differences
The main differences are, in my view, the following:

4.4.1.1. Horizontal versus sectoral approach
The proposed Directive on equal treatment in the provision of goods and services contains *horizontal* contract law provisions on sex discrimination

---

[134]   See for a similar view Basedow, Jürgen: The Renascence of Uniform Law, Europarättslig Tidskrift 1999 p 44.

[135]   See further www.sgecc.net/.

[136]   See further www.jus.unitn.it/dsg/common-core/approach.html.

[137]   See further www.acquis-group.org/index.html.

which (when/if adopted) will give legal form to the principle of gender equality in most areas of contract law. Existing EU contract law is, on the other hand, mainly based on a sectoral approach and the Action Plan favours a continuation of this approach.

4.4.1.2. Full harmonisation or minimum harmonisation

The trend in consumer protection law seems to be a move from minimum harmonisation towards full harmonisation, see for example the directive[138] on the protection of consumers in respect of distance contracts, which is a minimum directive, and the directive[139] concerning the distance marketing of consumer financial services which provides for full harmonisation.

The proposed Directive on equal treatment in the provision of goods and services is a minimum harmonisation directive which allows Member States to choose a higher standard of protection of the fundamental right of gender equality.

This difference is an expression of different attitudes to whether priority should be given to an internal market or a fundamental rights perspective. The smooth functioning of the internal market is generally better served by full harmonisation which abolish differences between the Member States than by minimum harmonisation.

The highest level of protection of fundamental rights can, however, be achieved by minimum harmonisation which allows individual Member States to choose a higher standard than the minimum required by EU law. In the proposal for the Directive on equal treatment in the provision of goods and services, [140] the Commission explicitly stresses that the EU approach to gender equality has developed over time, so that the original emphasis on avoiding distortions of competition between Member States has been replaced by a concern for equality as a fundamental right. In *Schröder*,[141] the ECJ similarly underlined the fundamental rights nature of equal pay as a reason for allowing Germany to prescribe a higher standard in German law than the minimum required by Article 141 EC.

4.4.1.3. Anchored in different parts of the Commission Services

The proposed Equality Directive is an initiative of the Commissioner for Employment and Social Affairs. The Action Plan on contract law is a joint

---

[138]   97/7/EC.

[139]   2002/65/EC.

[140]   COM(2003)657 p 2.

[141]   Case C-50/96, *Schröder* [2000] ECR I-743 paragraph 57.

initiative of the four Commissioners heading DG Sanco which is responsible for consumer and health issues, DG Markt which is responsible for the internal market, DG JAI which is responsible for the area of freedom, security and justice and DG Enterprise which is responsible for the EU enterprise policy which is aimed at promoting entrepreneurship and small and medium-sized enterprises.

4.4.1.4. Building on or disregarding employment law
In the comunication from July 2001 with which the Commission launched the current consultation process on contract law, it explicitly excluded employment law from the field. It stated:[142]

> In certain areas of private law, contracts are only one of the tools of regulation given the complexity of the relationship between the parties concerned. These areas, such as employment law and family law, give rise to particular issues and are not covered by this Communication.

The proposed equality Directive, on the other hand, builds on employment law and is in important respects, for example as regards basic concepts, identical with employment law directives.

4.4.2. Main similarities
The main similarities are, in my view, the following:

4.4.2.1. Not leaving the problems to be solved by the market
Because of the fundamental right nature of gender equality the economic reasons which may be invoked in favour of letting market forces deal with gender problems in the area of contract law are of less importance in the field of sex discrimination than in many other areas. The basic rules on gender equality in the *acquis communautaire* are mandatory and cannot be derogated from by contract.[143] With the high priority given to the fundamental rights perspective it is hardly surprising that the proposal for an equality Directive rejects the pssibility of leaving problems to be solved by the market. It is, perhaps, more surprising that the Action Plan on European contract law - with its high priority on the smooth functioning of the internal market and full harmonisation - also rejects the option of leaving problems to be solved by the market.

---

[142]   COM(2001)398 point 14 at p 6.

[143]   Morris, Gillian S: Fundamental rights: exclusion by agreement? Industrial Law Journal 2001 p 49.

68

4.4.2.2. Targeting the financial sector
Both documents see the financial sector as a key sector.

4.4.2.3. Focus on conceptual clarification
In respect of the concept of sex discrimination the proposal for an equality Directive contributes considerable to clarification of the concept. The Action Plan generally calls for conceptual clarification.

4.4.2.4. A move towards more coherence
The EU Commission's contributions to the current debate on European contract law call for more coherence. In the Action Plan the Commission seems to take for granted that more coherence in contract law will improve its quality. That is not always the case.[144] A fragmented legal system is typically an open, experimental, learning type of law whereas a more coherent legal system may fence off those aspects (for example gender) which are not (yet) fully understood at the time when the legal system is made coherent.

There is a risk that Community law is not yet mature enough to be restated as a gender mainstreamed coherent legal system. The law of surety contracts, discussed below in Chapter 4 in regard to surety wives, is an example of a fragmented area of contract law which is in the process of being transformed into a more coherent regulation. This example illustrates that when problems are addressed on a case by case basis the gender aspects become visible - at least in the most obvious cases - also for actors who are not generally experts in gender equality while the gender dimension may easily be overlooked when drafting a coherent rule if the drafters do not have sufficient skills in gender mainstreaming. That is a negative aspect of increased coherence.

Even though time may not be ripe for a general coherent restatement of contract law the situation is different in respect of establishing a coherent ban on sex discrimination. The general pattern is that the contract law provisions currently in force which explicitly or implicitly relate to gender are fragmentary and without internal coherence. To some - but very varying - extent there are duties both to gender mainstream and to abstain from sex discrimination spread around in the European contract law systems, both at national, EU and international level. Adoption of the pending proposal for a Directive on equal treatment in the provision of goods and services will reinforce, extend and generalise the prohibition against discrimination on grounds of sex in contract law which already exists in a number of Member States.

---

[144]   Wilhelmsson, Thomas: Private Law in the EU: Harmonised or Fragmented Europeanisation?, European Review of Private Law 2002 p 77 argues for a fragmented Europeanisation of private law.

Chapter 3

Basic Concepts

1. Introduction

One of the important consequences of increased EU involvement in gender equality contract law is that the basic concepts become Community concepts.

Those concepts have evolved over a period of approximately 30 years - first through ECJ case law on employment sex discrimination and free movement of workers - later through legislation on a number of discrimination issues.

In 2002, the Equal Treatment between Men and Women in Employment and Occupation Directive[1] was amended to consolidate the practice of the ECJ and to align it with the definitions of basic concepts used in the Race Discrimination Directive[2] and the Framework Employment Directive.[3] The proposal for a Directive on equal treatment between women and men in the provision of goods and services[4] takes over the basic concepts as defined in the Equal Treatment in Employment and Occupation Directive in almost identical terms.

In this chapter I discuss these concepts and their consequences when applied to contract law in matters other than employment. I particularly discuss whether different treatment of men and women for *commercial purposes* may be positive action and whether a commercial aim is a legitimate defence for direct or indirect sex discrimination.

2. Social Gender and Biological Sex

Gender equality law addresses problems related both to the treatment of social gender and biological sex. In modern business practice different treatment based on biological sex is probably on the way out while market segmentation by

---

[1]   2002/73/EC amending directive 76/207/EEC.

[2]   2000/43/EC. The directive has a broad scope of application including provision of goods and services.

[3]   2000/78/EC. The directive prohibits discrimination on grounds of religion, age, handicap and sexual orientation in employment. It does not apply to the provision of goods and services.

[4]   COM(2003)657.

gender is a standard element in professional marketing. In pace with increased professionalisation of business life gender differentiations therefore become more widespread and sophisticated.

In marketing literature there are warnings against confusing the use of gender as a segmentation basis with a classification based on sex. Palmer thus writes:[5]

> The latter is essentially a biological description, whereas *gender* is a social construct. Western societies have seen a convergence in many male and female values, although there remains argument about just how far this has gone. Many marketers have therefore moved on from segmentation based on a dichotomous male/female classification to a segmentation basis which recognizes a wide range of *gender* orientations. For example, the lifestyle and buying behaviour of career women is likely to be quite different from that of housewives. Many companies have developed marketing programmes which are aimed at segments of gay or lesbian people, whose buying behaviour may not fit neatly within dichotomous measures of *gender*.

See further on market segmentation by gender below in Chapter 4.

3. Formal and substantive equality

Substantive equality recognises that for individuals to receive equal treatment in practice they must often receive different or unequal treatment, see for example the wording of Article 141(4) EC on positive action which provides 'With a view to ensuring full equality in practice ....' .[6] Formal equality, on the other hand, forbids any form of discrimination in order to achieve equal treatment.

EU law on gender equality covers both substantive and formal equality. The ban on direct sex discrimination contributes mainly to securing formal equality while the ban on indirect sex discrimination, the mainstreaming strategy and positive action are mainly directed at achieving substantive equality. In *Kalanke*, AG Tesauro explained the concepts of substantive and formal equality in the following terms:[7]

> 16. The principle of substantive equality necessitates taking account of the existing inequalities which arise because a person belongs to a particular class of persons or to a particular social group; it enables and requires the unequal, detrimental effects which those inequalities have on the members of the group in question to be eliminated or, in any event, neutralized by means of specific measures.

---

[5]   Palmer, Adrian: Principles of Marketing, Oxford 2000 p 59.

[6]   See below in part 4 on positive action.

[7]   Case C-450/93, *Kalanke* [1995] ECR I-3051, point 16.

Unlike the principle of formal equality, which precludes basing unequal treatment of individuals on certain differentiating factors, such as sex, the principle of substantive equality refers to a positive concept by basing itself precisely on the relevance of those different factors themselves in order to legitimize an unequal right, which is to be used in order to achieve equality as between persons who are regarded not as neutral but having regard to their differences. In the final analysis, the principle of substantive equality complements the principle of formal equality and authorizes only such deviations from that principle as are justified by the end which they seek to achieve, that of securing actual equality. The ultimate objective is therefore the same: securing equality as between persons.

The approach of the EC Treaty to the gender factor is not only an anti-discrimination approach, but also increasingly - and particularly after the coming into force of the Amsterdam Treaty as at 1.5.1999 which placed the mainstreaming duty at Treaty level - a proactive, substantive equality approach. The appropriate action required by Article 13 EC - which is the legal basis of the proposed Directive on equal treatment in the provision of goods and services - is to combat sex discrimination. Other provisions like the mainstreaming provision in Article 3(2) and the positive action provision in Article 141(4) more directly pursue substantive gender equality. Article 3(2) EC provides that in all the activities referred to in this Article - that includes everything the EU has competence to do in matters of contract law - the Community shall aim to eliminate inequalities (not just combat discrimination), and to promote equality, between men and women. Article 141(4) EC refers to the aim of ensuring full equality in practice between men and women in working life and allows for some forms of specific positive action measures.

As mentioned in Chapter 1, the concept of indirect sex discrimination in employment was first developed in US/UK law and then spread around the EU through Community legislation.[8] In the further development of the gender equality concepts it seems that the EU and continental European countries[9] place

---

[8] See on the common law influence in employment discrimination law Thüsing, Gregor: Following the US Example: European Employment Discrimination Law and the Impact of Council Directives 2000/43/EC and 2000/78/EC, International Journal of Comparative Labour Law and Industrial Relations 2003 p 187. See generally on the similarities and differences between employment discrimination law in the EU and US Roseberry, Lynn: The Limits of Employment Discrimination Law in the United States and European Community, Copenhagen 1999.

[9] See further Schiek, Dagmar: Torn between Arithmetic and Substantive Equality? Perspectives on Equality in German Labour Law, The International Journal of Comparative Labour Law and Industrial Relations 2002 p 149.

greater weight on substantive equality than the US. As a result of a comparison between EU, Canada and the US, Totten thus argues (emphasis added):[10]

> While Canada, Germany and the European Union have increasingly supported notions of *substantive equality*, positive governmental duties and indirect discrimination in their gender equality jurisprudence, American constitutional jurisprudence in this area has largely espoused contrary notions of *formal equality*, negative duties and purposive-only discrimination.

4. The Gender Mainstreaming Strategy

The gender mainstreaming strategy is mainly addressed to the drafters of rules and policies at all levels in society, for example legislators, judges, organisations and businesses, and calls upon them to integrate the gender dimension into the design and implementation of all their rules and policies.

Under Article 3(2)EC there is an obligation for all Community actors (legislator, judiciary, executive) to contribute to gender mainstreaming European contract law when they participate in its development. At national level, the law on gender mainstreaming varies considerably from country to country. The amendment to the Equal Treatment Directive in 2002[11] extended the personal scope of the obligation to gender mainstream in matters of employment from Community actors to the Member States. There are broad gender mainstreaming duties for public authorities in (almost) all areas of society in the Nordic countries. In these countries public authorities taking part in the development of European contract law are therefore - like the Community actors - under an obligation to contribute to gender mainstreaming it. Private businesses, acting in other capacities than as employers, have, as the law stands at present, practically no legally binding duties of gender mainstreaming.

4.1. Definition(s) of the Concept of Gender Mainstreaming

The concept of gender mainstreaming is not clearly defined.[12] Many have used the metaphor of equality as something that flows in its own subsidiary stream. With the mainstreaming strategy equality is lifted into the main stream understood as the ordinary organisational, political and legal system.

---

[10] Totten, Christopher D: Constitutional Precommitments to Gender Affirmative Action in the European Union, Germany, Canada and the United States: A Comparative Approach, Berkeley Journal of International Law, 2003 p 27.

[11] 2002/73/EC.

[12] See generally on gender mainstreaming and the legal sources requiring or recommending it http://europa.eu.int/comm/employment_social/equ_opp/ gms_en.html.

In the current action plan for gender equality[13] it is - after noting that there are still structural gender inequalities - stated:

> This situation can be tackled efficiently by integrating the gender equality objective into the policies that have a direct or indirect impact on the lives of women and men. Women's concerns, needs and aspirations should be taken into account and assume the same importance as men's concerns in the design and implementation of policies. This is the gender mainstreaming approach, adopted in 1996 by the Commission[14]

In this programme the mainstreaming strategy is described as a pro-active strategy which integrates the gender aspect into all areas covered by Community competence and is complemented by specific actions with a view to enhance women's position in society. At the Commission's homepage on gender mainstreaming it states that its mainstreaming method consist of the following:[15]

Dual approach = gender mainstreaming + specific actions
Gender impact assessment & gender proofing
Mobilising all Commission services
Anchoring responsibility
Training for & awareness raising among key personnel
Monitoring, benchmarking and break down of data and statistics by sex
Structures:
        Group of Commissioners on Equal Opportunities,
        Inter-service Group on Gender Equality,
        Advisory Committee on Equal Opportunities for women and men

In the Council of Europe's report on mainstreaming from 1998[16] it is defined in the following way:

> Gender mainstreaming is the (re)organisation, improvement, development and evaluation of policy processes, so that a gender equality perspective is incorporated

---

[13] COM(2000)335, Community Framework Strategy on Gender Equality (2001-2005) available at http://europa.eu.int/comm/employment_social/equ_opp/strategy/2_en.html.

[14] COM(96)67, Commission Communication of 21 February 1996, Incorporating equal opportunities for women and men into all Community policies and activities.

[15] europa.eu.int/comm/employment_social/equ_opp/gms_en.html.

[16] Gender Mainstreaming. Conceptual framework, methodology and presentation of good practices, Strasbourg, May 1998, available at http://www.humanrights.coe.int/equality/

in all polices at all levels and at all stages, by the actors normally involved in policy-making.

It is further explained that gender mainstreaming can mean that the policy process is reorganised so that ordinary actors know how to incorporate a gender perspective. It can also mean that gender expertise is made a normal requirement for policy-makers.

4.2. Methods of Gender Mainstreaming

Gender mainstreaming implies that the gender dimension is made visible and taken into account at an early stage of the planning and design of rules and policies before anyone has actually suffered discrimination so that sex discrimination (direct and indirect discrimination, harassment and sexual harassment) is prevented from happening. There is no general agreement on how this should be done. Different actors use different methods, often of a socio-economic and not strictly legal nature.

4.2.1. Socio-economic methods
In Sweden the so-called 3R method has been widely discussed. It is a review and analysis tool[17] which serves as an aid in systematically compiling facts and information about the situations of women and men in a given operation or transaction. The three R's stand for Representation (how many women and how many men?), Resources (how are the resources – money, space and time – distributed between women and men?) and Realia (how come representation and resource distribution are divided between the sexes in the way they are?).

So far, the Commission has mainly pursued its gender mainstreaming strategy by means of gender-disaggregated statistical data, bench marking, gender impact assessments and socio-economic gender equality indicators.

As an example from socio-legal contract law research which highlights the social and economic gender-relatedness of the law of surety contracts Belinda Fehlberg's study on surety wives may be mentioned.[18]

4.2.2. Case law and academic legal literature
In my view traditional legal sources such as case law and academic literature will often be useful tools in making the gender dimension of a particular area of law visible. The issue of surety wives and their legal position has for example - in

---

[17] See further Just Progress! Applying gender mainstreaming in Sweden, http://naring.regeringen.se/pressinfo/infomaterial/pdf/N2001_052.pdf

[18] Fehlberg, Belinda: Sexually transmitted debt - Surety experience and English law, Oxford 1997.

addition to the abovementioned socio-legal study - also been addressed in traditional legal literature[19] and case law[20] on a number of occasions during recent years. The proposal for a Directive on credit for consumers from 2002[21] which will harmonise the law of consumer surety contracts does, however, not integrate the gender aspect, see further below in Chapter 4.

4.3. Fragmentary duty to gender mainstream European contract law

The mainstreaming principle was first applied in the context of international development aid where it has been used since the mid 1980's.[22]

4.3.1. The EU duty of gender mainstreaming
The EU has practised the gender mainstreaming strategy by means of soft law since the early 1990's in the field of employment and occupation and increasingly also in other fields such as development aid and research.[23] The first binding EU measure on gender mainstreaming was the Regulation on gender mainstreaming activities in the area of development cooperation.[24]

---

[19] See for example Debra Morris: Surety Wives in the House of Lords: Time for Solicitors to `Get Real'? *Royal Bank of Scotland plc* v. *Etridge (No. 2)* [2001] 4 All E.R. 449, Feminist Legal Studies 2003 p 57, Geary, David: Notes on Family Guarantees in English and Scottish Law - A Comment, European Review of Private Law 2000 p 25 and Fehlberg, Belinda: Sexually transmitted debt - Surety experience and English law, Oxford 1997.

[20] http://www.parliament.the-stationery-office.co.uk/pa/ld200102/ldjudgmt/jd011011/et ridg-1.htm, 11 October 2001 [2001] UKHL 44

[21] COM(2002)443.

[22] See further Razavi, Shahra og Carol Miller: Gender Mainstreaming. A Study on the Efforts by the UNDP, the World Bank and the ILO to Institutionalize Gender Issues, Occasional Paper Series, Fourth World Conference on Women, OP 4, UNRISD (United Nations Research Institute for Social Development), August 1995 and Programme of Action for the mainstreaming of gender equality in Community Development Co-operation COM(2001)295.

[23] See Council Resolution of 20 May 1999 on women and science, OJ 1999 C 201.

[24] Council Regulation (EC) No 2836/98 of 22 December 1998 on integrating of gender issues in development cooperation. This Regulation will expire in December 2003. In the Commission's work programme for 2003, COM (2002)590, it is announced that it will be revised taking into account the main elements of the Programme of Action for the mainstreaming of gender equality in Community Development Co-operation COM(2001)295.

The Community's mainstreaming obligation was (as from 1 May 1999) reinforced by the Amsterdam Treaty which elevated it in the hierarchy of the sources of law to Treaty level and extended its material scope to all areas covered by Community competence.

Under Article 2 EC, the Community shall have as its task to promote equality between men and women. Article 3(2) EC states that in the context of the activities referred to in Article 3(1) EC carried on for the purposes set out in Article 2 EC: 'the Community shall aim to eliminate inequalities, and to promote equality, between men and women.' In the Equal Treatment Directive as amended in 2002[25] these Treaty provisions are summarised as follows (emphasis added):

> Equality between women and men is a fundamental principle, under Article 2 and Article 3(2) of the EC Treaty and the case-law of the Court of Justice. These Treaty provisions proclaim equality between women and men as a "task" and an "aim" of the Community and impose a *positive obligation* to "promote" it in all its activities.

Article II-23 of the draft Constitution for the EU provides that equality between men and women must be ensured in all areas, including employment, work and pay. Article III-3 puts an obligation upon the Member States to integrate the aim to combat discrimination based on sex, racial or ethnic origin, religion or belief, disability, age or sexual orientation when defining and implementing all the policies and activities referred to in Part III of the draft Constitution.

4.3.2. Duty to take both sexes into account

Article I-26(2) of the draft Constitution[26] provides on the future composition of the Commission (emphasis added):

> Each Member State determined by the system of rotation shall establish a list of *three persons, in which both genders shall be represented,* whom it considers qualified to be a European Commissioner.

There is also EU soft law on equal participation of men and women, see for example the Council Resolution[27] on equal access to and participation of women and men in the knowledge society.

---

[25] Recital 4 of Directive 2002/73/EC.

[26] http://european-convention.eu.int/docs/Treaty/cv00850.en03.pdf.

[27] OJ 2003 C 317, Council Resolution of 27 November 2003 on equal access to and participation of women and men in the knowledge society for growth and innovation.

As a result of the above provisions there is an obligation for all Community actors (legislator, judiciary, executive) to contribute to gender mainstreaming European contract law when they participate in its development.

4.3.3. The ECJ

In *Dory*[28] AG Stix-Hackl argued that there is an obligation for the ECJ to interpret anti-discriminatory Community measures[29] in light of the mainstreaming provision in Article 3(2)EC, see the following:

> .. in my opinion, in interpreting the scope of Directive 76/207, Article 3(2) EC must now also be taken into account. That provision of primary law was not yet in force at the time when the directive was drawn up. However, the Community is now expressly required by that provision actively to promote equality between men and women. 103 As regards the scope of Article 3(2) EC, it may be seen that it applies to the Community's 'activities referred to' in Article 3(1) EC. Community law concerning the equal treatment of men and women in access to employment may be regarded as 'social policy' within the meaning of Article 3(1)(j) EC. (48) As regards the 'activities referred to', Article 3(2) EC imposes an obligation on 'the Community'. That presumably includes the Court when dealing, in connection with a reference for a preliminary ruling, with the interpretation of secondary law in the field of social policy.

That principle will apply equally or *a fortiori* to the coming Directive on equal treatment in the provision of goods and services. The coming Directive will be adopted at a time when the gender mainstreaming strategy is well-known and at least some of the participants in the legislative process are very conscious about the mainstreaming perspective in the proposed directive.

4.3.4. National courts' duty of gender mainstreaming under Community law

In 1984, in *Colson*,[30] and *Harz*,[31] the ECJ laid down an obligation for all the authorities of the Member States, and especially the courts, to interpret national

---

[28] Case C-186/01, *Alexander Dory* v *Deutschland* [2003] ECR I-2479, point 102-3.

[29] In *Dory* the old Equal Treatment Directive 76/207/EEC.

[30] Case 14/83 *Von Colson and Kamann* v *Land Nordrhein-Westfalen* [1984] ECR 1891.

[31] Case 79/83 *Dorit Harz* v *Deutsche Tradax GmbH* [1984] ECR 1921.

law in conformity with Community law. AG Mancini, in *Jongeneel Kaas* described the national courts also as Community courts, see the following:[32]

> The general principles ... of Community law ... may be relied upon by individuals before the national court which, as is well known, is also a Community court.

AG Léger in *Köbler*[33] similarly stated that the European Communities have been developed and consolidated essentially through law. Since the national courts have the function of applying the law, including Community law, they inevitably constitute an essential cog in the Community legal order.

Because all national courts are, under EU law, also Community courts the national courts presumably have mainstreaming obligations similar to those of the ECJ.

4.3.5. Gender mainstreaming duties provided for in national law

At national level, the law on gender mainstreaming varies considerably from country to country. There are broad gender mainstreaming duties for public authorities in (almost) all areas of society in the Nordic countries.[34] In Germany,[35] Article 3 II of the Constitution has since its adoption in 1949 provided that ' Männer und Frauen sind gleichberechtigt.' This provision was amended in 1994 and the following sentence added to Article 3 II:

> (2) .... Der Staat fördert die tatsächliche Durchsetzung der Gleichberechtigung von Frauen und Männern und wirkt auf die Beseitigung bestehender Nachteile hin.

In these countries public authorities taking part in the development of European contract law are therefore - like the Community actors - under an obligation to contribute to gender mainstreaming it.

---

[32] Case 237/82, *Jongeneel Kaas* [1984] ECR 483.

[33] Case C-224/01, *Köbler* [2003] ECR I-00000 (nyr).

[34] See section 4 of the Finnish Equality Act (available in Swedish at http://www.tasa-arvo.fi/www-sve/lagstiftning/lagstiftning3.html) and section 4 of the Danish Equality Act, available in English at http://ligestillinguk.itide.dk/ Default.asp-?Id=194. See for Sweden, where the legal provisions are spread, Just Progress! Applying gender mainstreaming in Sweden, http://naring.regeringen.se/ pressinfo/infomaterial/pdf/N2001_ 052.pdf.

[35] See on German law Schiek, Dagmar et al: Frauengleichstellungsgesetze des Bundes und der Länder, Frankfurt am Main 2002.

The above provisions have probably no horizontal effect. Private businesses, acting in other capacities than as employers, have therefore, as the law stands at present, only limited duties to practise gender mainstreaming.[36]

In Norway, the government presented a bill to Parliament (the Storting) on 13 June 2003, proposing a requirement of at least forty per cent representation of both sexes on the boards of all state owned enterprises and public limited companies in the private sector. The new legislation is not intended to come into effect in the private sector if the desired gender balance is achieved voluntarily in the course of 2005. The rules applying to state-owned companies came into force on 1 January 2004.[37]

5. Positive action

As examples of relevant positive action measures in respect of contracts for the provision of goods and services, the Commission, in the proposal for a Directive on equal treatment in this area, mentions[38] women's difficulties in getting access to commercial loans and venture capital. While the application of the principle of equal treatment is likely to help with this situation, it is, in the view of the Commission, unlikely to be sufficient on its own to overcome the accumulated disadvantage faced by women. One response to this situation has been the establishment of specific loans for women entrepreneurs, at special rates or conditions, and the provision of extra business support and advice services for women entrepreneurs. Special services for women entrepreneurs exist in a number of Member States and in at least one, special banks or lending facilities exist specifically for this purpose. The Commission believes that the Directive should not prohibit the possibility for such measures in Member States and therefore that it is necessary to include an option for Member States to provide for positive action.

---

[36] The Norwegian Equality Act section 1a(3) provides: Enterprises that are subject to a statutory duty to prepare an annual report shall in the said report give an account of the actual state of affairs as regards gender equality in the enterprise. An account shall also be given of measures that have been implemented and measures that are planned to be implemented in order to promote gender equality and to prevent differential treatment in contravention of this Act. See also below in Chapter 4 on gender parity provisions with regard to Norwegian company boards.

[37] See further http://odin.dep.no/bfd/.

[38] COM(2003)756 p 14.

5.1. Division of power between the EU and the Member States

Positive action is an option for the Member States. There is never a duty under EU law for the Member States to take positive action or to allow or impose a duty upon their businesses/citizens to take positive action.

To some extent EU law prohibits positive action, namely proclaimed positive action measures that do not pursue a genuine equality purpose or apply excessive means to achieve its (lawful) purpose. If measures are within the sphere of lawful positive action under EU law it is for the Member States, in accordance with their political choices, to decide whether or not to allow or prohibit positive action in the individual country.

Under UK law, positive action is, in general, not lawful. There are limited exceptions allowing discrimination in training, or encouragement to apply for particular work in which members of the relevant sex are under-represented. The other EU/EEA countries with specific equality legislation applying to the provision of goods and services (ie Norway, Finland, Netherlands, Ireland, Denmark and Belgium, see above in chapter 2) allow positive action to some degree.

5.2. EU law

5.2.1. Statutory positive action provisions in EU law

Article 141(4) EC which applies to working life provides:

> 4. With a view to ensuring full equality in practice between men and women in working life, the principle of equal treatment shall not prevent any Member State from maintaining or adopting measures providing for specific advantages in order to make it easier for the underrepresented sex to pursue a vocational activity or to prevent or compensate for disadvantages in professional careers.

Article II-23 of the draft Constitutional Treaty which applies in all areas of law, also outside of employment[39] provides:

> Equality between men and women must be ensured in all areas, including employment, work and pay.
> The principle of equality shall not prevent the maintenance or adoption of measures providing for specific advantages in favour of the under-represented sex.

---

[39] Article 141(4) EC will, once the Constitutional Treaty has come into force, be replaced by Article III-108(4) of the Constituional Treaty which is identical with Article 141(4) EC.

Article 5 of the proposed Directive on equal treatment in the provision of goods and services provides on Positive action that

the principle of equal treatment shall not prevent any Member State from maintaining or adopting specific measures to prevent or compensate for disadvantages linked to sex.

Following the model of Race Discrimination Directive[40] this article confirms that the Member States may maintain or introduce specific measures to compensate for certain disadvantages accumulated by individuals of either sex in the field of goods and services. Such measures must be shown to be necessary, focussed on overcoming a specific disadvantage and must be limited in time, being in force no longer than is necessary to deal with the problem identified.

5.2.2. The case law of the ECJ
Article 2(4) of the Equal Treatment Directive 1976[41] provides:

4. This Directive shall be without prejudice to measures to promote equal opportunity for men and women, in particular by removing existing inequalities which affect women's opportunities in the areas referred to in Article 1(1)

Article 141(4) EC as worded by the Amsterdam Treaty provides

4. With a view to ensuring full equality in practice between men and women in working life, the principle of equal treatment shall not prevent any Member State from maintaining or adopting measures providing for specific advantages in order to make it easier for the under-represented sex to pursue a vocational activity or to prevent or compensate for disadvantages in professional careers.

The EC Treaty overrides the Equal Treatment Directive as lex superior. As the Commission stated in its proposal for an amendment of the Equal Treatment Directive,[42] Article 2(4) of the Directive has become redundant.[43] The Commission therefore proposed that it should be deleted.

---

[40] 2000/43/EC, paragraph 2.

[41] 76/207/EEC.

[42] COM(2000) 334.

[43] As at 1.5.1999 when the Amsterdam Treaty came into force.

Article 2(4) of the directive was interpreted by the ECJ in the *Commission v France*[44] case, the *Kalanke*[45] case and the *Marschall*[46] case and more recently in the *Badek*[47] case. The commission summarised that case law in the following way in the proposal for amendment of the Equal Treatment Directive:

- the possibility to adopt positive action measures is to be regarded as an exception to the principle of equal treatment;
- the exception is specifically and exclusively designed to allow for measures which, although discriminatory in appearance, are in fact intended to eliminate or reduce actual instances of inequality which may exist in the realit y of social life;
- automatic priority to women, as regards access to employment or promotion, in sectors where they are under-represented cannot be justified;
- conversely, such a priority is justified, if it is not automatic and if the national measure in question guarantees equally qualified male candidates that their situation will be the subject of an objective assessment which take into account all criteria specific to the candidates, whatever their gender.

The *Commission v France* case of 1986 is so far the only infringement procedure concerning positive action that has been brought before the ECJ. France had introduced a provision in the Code de Travail prescribing that any term reserving the benefit of any measure to one or more employees on grounds of sex included in any collective labour agreement or employment contract shall be void, except where such a clause was intended to implement provisions relating to pregnancy, nursing or pre-natal and post-natal rest. However, another provision prescribed that the above-mentioned provision of the Code de Travail did not prohibit the application of usages, terms of contracts of employment or collective agreements in force on the date on which the law was promulgated granting special rights to women. The Commission submitted – and was not contradicted by the French Government – that special rights for women included in collective agreements related in particular to: the extension of maternity leave; the shortening of working hours, for example for women over 59 years of age; the advancement of the retirement age; the obtaining of leave when a child was ill; the granting of additional days of annual leave in respect of each child: the granting of one day's leave at the beginning of the school year: the

---

[44] Case 312/86, *Commission v France* [1988] ECR 6315.

[45] Case C-450/93, *Kalanke* [1995] ECR I-3051.

[46] Case C-409/95, *Marschall* [1997] ECR I-6363.

[47] Case C-158/97, *Badeck* [2000] ECR I-1875 .

granting of time off work on Mother's Day; daily breaks for women working on keyboard equipment or employed as typists or switchboard operators; the granting of extra points for pension rights in respect of the second and subsequent children; and the payment of an allowance to mothers who had to meet the costs of nurseries or childminders.

The Commission accepted that some of those special rights may fall within the scope of the derogations in the Equal Treatment Directive. It submitted, however, that the French legislation, by its generality, made it possible to preserve for an indefinite period measures discriminating as between men and women contrary to the directive. The ECJ accepted the Commission's views on these points and France was ordered to amend its legislation.

The objection to the provision at issue was mainly that it was general and applied for an indefinite period. Thus, France had gone beyond what was necessary and had thus violated the principle of proportionality.

The interpretation of the new provision in Article 141(4) was addressed by the ECJ *Abrahamsson*[48] case. The ECJ confirmed that positive action aiming to promote women in those sectors of the public service where they are under-represented has to be considered as compatible with EU law. It clarified the conditions in which positive action can be applied and stated that the male and the female candidates must have equal or almost equal merits. The automatic and absolute preference of a candidate of the underrepresented sex who had a sufficient but lower qualification was by contrast incompatible with the principle of equal treatment.

Schnorbus[49] concerned the automatic preference accorded to male candidates who had completed compulsory military or civilian service for (all) positions as legal adviser in Land Hessen, Germany. The German court asked the ECJ:

> "4. Is the fact that the rule automatically results in the preferential admission of men to training without a decision on the matter being subject to an assessment of the individual circumstances or of other relevant factors meriting consideration in the interests of the remaining applicants sufficient to preclude justification of the rule under Article 2 (4) of Directive 76/207/EEC because it is to that extent more than a measure to promote equal opportunity?"

The ECJ established that a measure that accords preference to persons who have completed compulsory military or civilian service constitutes indirect discrimination in favour of men. The ECJ found however that the provision at issue, which took account of the delay experienced in the progress of their

---

[48] Case C-407/98, *Abrahamsson* [2000] ECR I-5539.

[49] Case C-79/99 *Schnorbus* [2000] ECR I-10997.

education by applicants who had been required to do military or civilian service, was objective in nature and prompted solely by the desire to counterbalance to some extent the effects of that delay. The automatic preference accorded to men was therefore not regarded as contrary to the Equal Treatment Directive. Judged on the basis of the principle of proportionality, the preference accorded to men did not go beyond what was necessary to compensate for the disadvantages entailed by compulsory military or community service.

Beyond the preference accorded to men who had completed compulsory military or civilian service, there was a possibility of taking particular hardship into account. This must be viewed in connection with the fact that the measure concerned all the positions as legal adviser in Land Hessen.

The *Lommers* case[50] concerned a Netherlands scheme under which the Minister for Agriculture made available subsidized nursery places to female officials. Women were given priority with regard to all the nursery places made available by the employer save in the event of an emergency, to be determined by the Minister. Thus, men could only obtain a nursery place from the employer in question if there was an emergency. In this case the ECJ made explicit reference to the principle of proportionality and established[51] that in cases involving preliminary questions it is, in principle, the task of the national court to ensure that the principle of proportionality is duly observed. However, the ECJ may provide the national court with an interpretation of Community law on all such points as may enable the court to assess the compatibility of a national measure with Community law. The Netherlands scheme was regarded as compatible with the Equal Treatment Directive.

To sum up, the ECJ disallowed positive action measures in the *Commission v France*, *Kalanke* and *Abrahamsson*, and approved such measures in *Marschall, Badeck, Schnorbus* and *Lommers*. Positive action is unlawful if the measure is very general and applies for an indefinite period, or if the method selected is disproportionate to the aim pursued (Abrahamsson). There is considerable latitude for applying gender quota arrangements when appointing people to training places/positions (Badeck). Although priority may be given automatically to one sex as regards access to employment and working conditions, eg nursery places (Schnorbus and Lommers), the opposite sex must not be excluded from all possibilities of obtaining a position or a working condition of the kind concerned (Kalanke, Marschall, Lommers).

---

[50] Case C-476/99, *Lommers* [2002] ECR I-2891.

[51] In paragraph 40.

5.3. The principle of proportionality

The general principle underlying ECJ case-law on positive action is that the principle of proportionality shall be observed. This means that any special measures that favour one sex shall serve a lawful purpose, they shall be appropriate and necessary for the attainment of this goal, and they must not go beyond what is necessary to attain it.

5.4. Purpose. Promotion of equality or sales promotion

In order for positive action measures to be lawful their purpose must be to ensure equality between men and women or as Article 141(4) expresses it 'full equality in practice.' The freedom to take positive action cannot be invoked when differential treatment of men and women is practised for commercial purposes. This may be illustrated by the Irish *Icon Night Club* case.

The case concerned a claim by a man that he was discriminated against by the Icon Night Club on grounds of sex when he was charged an entrance fee to the night club while at the same time females were allowed in free. The night club proprietor explained about the facts of the case that females were allowed in free up to 1am on a Thursday night and males were charged an entrance fee of £5. This policy was adopted for promotional reasons and had proved very successful in attracting females to the club. In July, 2001 he opened a bar attached to the nightclub and decided to run soccer nights on Monday night. Any male who came into the bar to watch soccer was let into the nightclub free. He discontinued the practice after about 2 months because it was not successful.

The Icon Night Club submitted that free entrance for women to the night club on Thursday nights was positive action for women and as such allowed under the Irish Equal Status Act Section 14(b)(i) which provides that nothing in the Act shall be construed as prohibiting

> (b) preferential treatment or the taking of positive measures which are bona fide intended to
> (i) promote equality of opportunity for persons who are, in relation to other persons, disadvantaged or who have been or are likely to be unable to avail themselves of the same opportunities as those other persons,

The Irish Equality Officer found,[52] that the action of the respondent was *not* a positive measure allowed under Section 14 of the Irish Equal Status Act, but was a measure taken for commercial reasons aimed at attracting more customers to

---

[52] The decision is available at www.odei.ie/2004%20Equal%20Status/DEC-S2004-001.pdf

the business, see further on the unlawfulness of charging different prices for men and women below in Chapter 4.

5.5. Specific advantages in favour of the under-represented sex

In the proposed Directive on equal treatment in the provision of goods and services provides the wording is 'specific measures to prevent or compensate for disadvantages linked to sex'. This wording indicates that the advantages accorded to one sex cannot be of a very general nature.

5.6. Is a provision on positive action a derogation from the principle of equal treatment or a clarification of the concept of gender equality?

It may be argued that positive action within the meaning of Article 141 (4) EC, as it is worded subsequent to the Amsterdam Treaty, must be regarded as a clarification of the concept of gender equality, not as a derogation from the principle of equal treatment. This is important with regard to interpretation, as derogations from fundamental principles are generally interpreted restrictively in Community law, whereas this is not the case with the clarification of concepts.

In *Kalanke*,[53] the ECJ pointed out that Article 2 (4) of the Equal Treatment Directive[54] is a derogation clause and must therefore be interpreted restrictively. This view has presumably not been relevant in the EU since the Amsterdam Treaty entered into force on 1 May 1999.

In favour of the above interpretation, CEDAW may also be referred to. So far, CEDAW has only played a limited role in Community law. There is however, reference to it in the preambles to all the discrimination directives adopted or proposed since 2000, ie the directive on race,[55] the framework directive (which prohibits discrimination on grounds of religion, age, handicap and sexual orientation in employment),[56] the directive on equal treatment for men and

---

[53] Case C-450/93, *Kalanke* [1995] ECR I-3051.

[54] 76/207/EEC.

[55] 2000/43/EC.

[56] 2000/78/EC.

88

women in employment and occupation[57] and the pending proposal for a Directive on equal treatment of men and women in the provision of goods and services.[58]

6. The principle of equal treatment

6.1. Overview of statutory definitions

The principle of equal treatment of women and men is explicitly referred to in CEDAW, in EU legislation and ECJ case law and in (many) national constitutions and national equality acts. Explicit references to the principle of equal treatment are, however, almost absent in gender-neutral sources of contract law such as the Nordic Contracts Acts or Sale of Goods Acts and the German Civil Code (BGB).[59]

Sex discrimination is prohibited with regard to practically all aspects of employment and occupation both at national, international and EUlevel.[60] All traditional sources of law (legislation, case law, scholarly writing) are used in employment discrimination law.

For the purposes of the proposed Directive on equal treatment in the access to and supply of goods and services,[61] the principle of equal treatment between men and women shall, according to Article 3, mean that

(a) there shall be no direct discrimination based on sex, including less favourable treatment of women for reasons of pregnancy and maternity;
(b) there shall be no indirect discrimination based on sex.

---

[57] 2002/73/EC.

[58] Recital 2 in COM(2003)756.

[59] The French Code Civil art 8 provides 'Tout Français jouira des droits civils'.

[60] See for a list of the relevant provisions at EU level the Commission=s web site on gender equality legislation at http://europa.eu.int/comm/employment_social/ equ_opp/rights_en.html and for details on the Member States the General reports of the Legal Experts' Group on Equal Treatment of Men and Women for 1997 and 1998 and for the following years Bulletin - Legal issues in Equality published three times a year, available at http://europa.eu.int/comm/employment_social/equ_opp/ rights-_en.html#let.

[61] COM(2003)657, Proposal to the European Parliament and the Council for a Council Directive implementing the principle of equal treatment between women and men in the access to and supply of goods and services, presented 5.11.2003. See also SEC(2003)1213, Commission Staff Working Paper which contains an Extended Impact Assessment of the proposal.

2. Harassment and sexual harassment within the meaning of this Directive shall be deemed to be discrimination on the grounds of sex and therefore prohibited. A person's rejection of, or submission to, such conduct may not be used as a basis for a decision affecting that person.

In contract matters other than employment there are only few and scattered rules on sex discrimination, mainly found in legislation. There is only scant case law and mainstream academic writing on contract law has by and large overlooked the ban on sex discrimination in the access to and supply of goods and services, also in countries like Belgium, Denmark, Finland, Ireland, the Netherlands, Norway and the UK where there are (general) statutory bans on such discrimination.

The concept of sex discrimination has been developed through case law, academic writing and legislation over the last 20-30 years, primarily in the field of employment and occupation.

Article 1 of CEDAW provides:

For the purposes of the present Convention, the term 'discrimination against women' shall mean any distinction, exclusion or restriction made on the basis of sex which has the effect or purpose of impairing or nullifying the recognition, enjoyment or exercise by women, irrespective of their marital status, on a basis of equality of men and women, of human rights and fundamental freedoms in the political, economic, social, cultural, civil or any other field.

Sex discrimination is defined in Community legislation as covering direct and indirect discrimination and harassment and sexual harassment. Article 3 of the proposed Directive on equal treatment in the provision of goods and services[62] explains the meaning of the application of the principle of equal treatment. It specifies that the principle of equal treatment between men and women shall mean that there shall be no direct discrimination based on sex, including unfavourable treatment of women for reasons of pregnancy and maternity, nor indirect discrimination based on sex. In this context, as in the earlier Directive, harassment and sexual harassment are also to be considered discrimination based on sex.

For the purposes of the proposed Directive on equal treatment in the access to and supply of goods and services, the following definitions shall according to Article 2, apply:

---

[62] COM(2003)657, Proposal to the European Parliament and the Council for a Council Directive implementing the principle of equal treatment between women and men in the access to and supply of goods and services, presented 5.11.2003. See also SEC(2003)1213, Commission Staff Working Paper which contains an Extended Impact Assessment of the proposal.

(a) direct discrimination occurs where one person is treated less favourably, on grounds of sex, than another is, has been or would be treated in a comparable situation;

(b) indirect discrimination occurs where an apparently neutral provision, criterion or practice would put persons of one sex at a particular disadvantage compared with persons of the other sex, unless that provision, criterion or practice is objectively justified by a legitimate aim and the means of achieving that aim are appropriate and necessary;

(c) harassment occurs where unwanted conduct related to the sex of a person is exhibited with the purpose or effect of violating the dignity of a person and of creating an intimidating, hostile, degrading, humiliating or offensive environment;

(d) sexual harassment occurs where unwanted physical, verbal or non-verbal conduct of a sexual nature is exhibited with the purpose or effect of violating the dignity of a person and of creating an intimidating, hostile, degrading, humiliating or offensive environment;

2. Incitement to direct or indirect discrimination on grounds of sex shall be deemed to be discrimination within the meaning of this Directive.

The definitions are drawn from existing Community law and do not depart from previously agreed approaches.[63] The concepts of direct and indirect discrimination and sex-based and sexual harassment are, *mutatis mutandis*, identical to those contained in the already existing Article 13 Directives from 2000[64] and the amended Equal Treatment Directive from 2002[65]

The only important difference is that the prohibition against 'instructions' to discriminate has been changed into a prohibition against 'incitements'[66] to discriminate.

6.2. Comparisons

6.2.1. Differences must be attributable to a single source
Where the contested differences in treatment of men and women cannot be attributed to a single source, there is no body which is responsible for the

---

[63] COM(2003)756 p 13.

[64] 2000/43/EC on race discrimination which in addition to employment applies *inter alia* to contracts for the provision of goods and services and the employment framework directivve 2000/78/EC on discrimination on grounds of religion, age, handicap and sexual orientation.

[65] 2002/73/EC.

[66] In the other language versions there is a similar shift in meaning: in French from 'Tout comportement consistant à enjoindre' to 'l'incitation à la discrimination', in German from Anwisung to Aufforderung and in Danish from instruktion to tilskyndelse.

inequality and which could restore equal treatment. It is settled case law that such situations do not come within the scope of the equal pay provision in Article 141(1) EC.[67] The same principle must apply in matters outside of the labour market.

What can be compared are different treatment of men and women in legislation, branch rules and collective contracts or the contracts of one business with its business partners or customers. The fact that one business may treat men differently from the way another business treats women is not discrimination within the meaning of the gender equality rules.

6.2.2. Discrimination on grounds of pregnancy

It is settled case law[68] that when a woman is discriminated against on grounds of pregnancy it is irrelevant whether there is a male comparator.

6.2.3. Hypothetical comparator

The last part of the definition in the proposed Directive Article 2(a) - one person is treated less favourably than another *would be* treated - shows that a comparison can be made with a hypothetical comparator. This is an important precision because the question whether and to what extent hypothetical comparators may be used is a vexed issue in employment discrimination law.

The ECJ's judgment in Macarthys[69] is often interpreted as preventing a woman from comparing herself with a hypothetical man. The ECJ was requested to rule upon a submission made by the respondent to the effect that a woman may claim not only the salary received by a man who previously did the same work for her employer but also, more generally, the salary to which she would be entitled were she a man, even in the absence of any man who was concurrently performing, or had previously performed, similar work. The respondent in the main action defined this term of comparison by reference to the concept of what she described as 'a hypothetical male worker'. The Court ruled on this problem:

> 15. It is clear that the latter proposition... is to be classed as indirect and disguised discrimination, the identification of which, as the court explained in the Defrenne judgment.... implies comparative studies of entire branches of industry and therefore requires, as a prerequisite, the elaboration by the community and national legislative bodies of criteria of assessment. From that it follows that, in cases of actual discrimination falling within the scope of the direct application of Article 119 [now after amendment Article 141 EC], comparisons are confined to parallels which may

---

[67] Case C-320/00, *Lawrence and Others* [2002] ECR I-7325, paragraph 17 and Case C-256/01, *Allonby* [2004] ECR 00000 (nyr, judgment of 13.1.2004).

[68] See for example Case C-177/88,*Dekker* [1990] ECR I-3941.

[69] Case 129/79, *Macarthys* [1980] ECR 1275.

be drawn on the basis of concrete appraisals of the work actually performed by employees of different sex within the same establishment or service.

In *Barber*,[70] the ECJ held (emphasis added) that Article 141 EC applies directly to all forms of discrimination which may be identified solely with the aid of the criteria of equal work and equal pay referred to by that provision, without national or Community measures being required to define them with greater precision . The national court before which that provision is relied upon must safeguard the rights which it confers on individuals, in particular where a private occupational pension scheme which operates in part as a substitute for the statutory scheme refuses to pay to a man on redundancy an immediate pension such as would be granted in a similar case to a woman .

McCrudden holds the view that there is no right under UK law for a woman to compare herself with a hypothetical male.[71]

6.2.4. Overall assessment or point by point comparison

In *Barber*,[72] the Court of Appeal in England asked whether equal pay must be ensured at the level of each element of remuneration or only on the basis of a comprehensive assessment of the consideration paid to workers.

The ECJ emphasized the fundamental importance of *transparency* and, in particular, of the possibility of a review by the national courts, in order to prevent and, if necessary, eliminate any discrimination based on sex. With regard to the means of verifying compliance with the principle of equal pay, it must be stated that if the national courts were under an obligation to make an assessment and a comparison of all the various types of consideration granted, according to the circumstances, to men and women, judicial review would be difficult and the effectiveness of Article 141 EC would be diminished as a result. It follows that genuine transparency, permitting an effective review, is assured only if the principle of equal pay applies to each of the elements of remuneration granted to men or women. The answer was therefore that it is contrary to Article 141 EC for a man made compulsorily redundant to be entitled to claim only a deferred pension payable at the normal pensionable age when a woman in the same position is entitled to an immediate retirement pension as a result of the application of an age condition that varies according to sex in the same way as is provided for by the national statutory pension scheme. The Court held (emphasis added):

---

[70] Case C-262/88 *Barber* [1990] ECR I-1889.

[71] McCrudden, Christopher: Equality in Law between Men and Women in the European Community, United Kingdom, Luxembourg 1994 p 42.

[72] Case C-262/88 *Barber* [1990] ECR-I-1889.

With regard to equal pay for men and women, *genuine transparency*, permitting an effective review by the national court, is assured only if the principle of equal pay must be observed in respect of each of the elements of remuneration granted to men and women, and not on a comprehensive basis in respect of all the consideration granted to men and women.

In *Jämställdhetsombudsmannen*[73] the Swedish Labour Court asked whether an inconvenient-hours supplement and the reduction in working time awarded in respect of work performed according to a three-shift roster as compared to normal working time for day-work, or the value of that reduction, are to be taken into consideration in calculating the salary which serves as the basis for a pay comparison for the purpose of Article 141 EC and the Equal Pay Directive.

The answer was no. The fact that midwives who are predominantly female often do work at inconvenient hours or shift work and thereby, when they add their basic wages and the supplements they receive to compensate for inconveniences, obtain the same average wages as clinical technicians who are predominantly male and only do day work, does not preclude pay discrimination.

Under EU law the basic wages must be compared without increments for inconvenient hours and shift work being taken into account. The reason is that if the national courts were under an obligation to make an assessment and a comparison of all the various types of consideration granted, according to the circumstances, to men and women, judicial review would be difficult and the effectiveness of Article 141 EC would be diminished as a result.

The *Jørgensen* case[74] was basically about the same problem as the *JämO* case but not in an equal pay case but in a dispute in the independent professions between a female practising doctor (a rheumatologist), on the one hand, and the Danish Association of Specialized Medical Practitioners and the National Health Insurance Negotiations Committee, on the other hand, concerning the application of a negotiated scheme for the reorganization of medical practices in Denmark.

The Østre Landsret asked the ECJ to clarify how an assessment as to whether there is indirect discrimination on grounds of sex should be undertaken in a case concerning equal treatment.[75] The Danish Court considered it settled case-law on equal pay that a point-for-point comparison should be made, and asked the ECJ to clarify whether the comparison of occupational conditions to be undertaken in an equal treatment case in the independent professions should be also made by way of a point-for-point comparison as in equal pay cases or could

---

[73] Case C-236/98 *Jämställdhetsombudsmannen* [2000] ECR I-2189.

[74] Case C-226/98, *Jørgensen* [2000] ECR I-2447.

[75] Under Directive 76/207/EEC and Directive 86/613/EEC.

be made by way of an overall assessment of all the surrounding factors. It informed the ECJ that it could be assumed in answering the question that the negotiated reorganisation scheme, assessed as a whole, is gender-neutral in both its effect and purpose. It could further be assumed that the negotiated reorganisation scheme contained provisions which, viewed in isolation, result in a sex bias, inasmuch as it appeared that some provisions predominantly affected female specialised medical practitioners whilst other provisions predominantly affected male specialised medical practitioners.

The ECJ referred to its judgment in *Barber* where it relied on the principle of effectiveness and transparency, see above, and stated that the same finding applies to all aspects of the principle of equal treatment and not only to those which have a bearing on equal pay.

It is thus a general principle that overall comparisons showing a balance between the advantages obtained by women and men cannot justify differences in regard to specific elements. Equal pay and equal treatment must be observed in respect of each of the elements of the working conditions. The same principle must apply to contract outside of the labour market.

7. Direct Sex Discrimination

According to Article 2(a) of the proposed Directive on equal treatment in the provision of goods and services direct discrimination occurs where one person is treated less favourably, on grounds of sex, than another is, has been or would be treated in a comparable situation and according to Article 3 the principle of equal treatment between men and women shall mean that there shall be no direct discrimination based on sex, including less favourable treatment of women for reasons of pregnancy and maternity.

7.1. Different treatment on the basis of different expectations

In matters of equal pay in employment, it is settled case law that different expectations on grounds of sex can be no ground for differences in pay to women and men for work still to be performed. In *Brunnhofer*,[76] the ECJ thus held that in the case of work paid at time rates, a difference in pay awarded, at the time of their appointment, to two employees of different sex for the same job or work of equal value cannot be justified by factors which become known only after the employees concerned take up their duties and which can be assessed only once the employment contract is being performed, such as a difference in the individual work capacity of the persons concerned or in the

---

[76] Case C-381/99, *Brunnhofer* [2001] ECR I-4961.

effectiveness of the work of a specific employee compared with that of a colleague.

The same principle must apply to other contracts. Differential treatment of men and women in early stages of a contractual process cannot be justified by reference to expected differences in the behaviour of men and women at later stages of the contractual process.

7.2. Right to individual treatment. Prohibition against group treatment

As set out above the Equal Treatment in Employment Directive and the proposed Directive on Equal Treatment in the provision of goods and services define direct sex discrimination as a situation where *one person* is treate d less favourably on grounds of sex than another is, has been or would be treated in a comparable situation (emphasis added).

Under the Equal Treatment Directive the ban on sex discrimination confers a right on each man and each woman to be treated on an individual basis irrespective of the general characteristics of the gender group they belong to, also in situations where an employer's assumptions about the different gender group's characteristics are empirically true. No individual man can, for example, be refused a job which requires dexterity just because women on average are better in that respect and no individual woman can be turned down for a job which requires physical strength just because men on average are stronger. A potential employer must assess job applicants on their individual merits.

Persons seeking to obtain other contracts than employment contracts, eg insurance contracts and pension contracts, are probably often subjected to group assessments, ie a treatment which amounts to direct sex discrimination as defined in the Equal Treatment Directive.

One of the obvious group differences between men and women is that women in EU Member States on average live longer than men. In a number of EU countries occupational pension schemes must use unisex calculations.[77] Article 4 of the the proposed Directive on equal treatment in the access to and supply of goods and services provides specifically targets discrimination by reference to actuarial factors, see further below in Chapter 4.

---

[77] See for details Joint report by the Commission and the Council on adequate and sustainable pensions, March 2003, available at http://europa.eu.int/comm/employment_social/soc-prot/pensions/2003jpr_en.pdf.

7.3. Sex+. Discrimination against subgroups of women or men

Many cases of discrimination consist in unfavourable treatment of subgroups of women or subgroups of men. The targeted persons are not selected exclusively on grounds of sex but on grounds of sex + something more.

Among women pregnant women, single mothers and mothers of small children are probably those who are most exposed to discrimination. In the Staff Working Paper[78] on the proposed directive on equal treatment in the access to and supply of goods and services refusal to provide a mortgage to pregnant women is mentioned as an example of discrimination that has been reported to the Commission. As mentioned in Chapter 1 one of the respondents in an analysis by the Danish Agency for Trade and Industry stated[79] that single mothers do not have much chance of obtaining a loan for their enterprises. The proposed Directive on equal treatment in the provision of goods and services explicitly classifies less favourable treatment of women for reasons of pregnancy and maternity as direct discrimination.

For men sex discrimination often occurs in combination with age, eg discrimination against young men in car insurance or - mainly in countries where state social security is based on different pension ages for men and women - discrimination against older men who have passed the pension age for women but not reached the pension age for their own sex, see further below in chapter 4 on sex-based price differences. In the UK - where the state pension age at the material time was 60 for women and 65 for men - the House of Lords has decided a case where a married man who was 61 wanted to visit a swimming pool together with his wife who was also 61. She was admitted free of charge because she had passed the pension age while he was required to pay an admission fee because he had not passed the pension age. This was held to be unlawful under the UK Sex Discrimination Act 1975.[80]

---

[78] SEC(2003)1213 p 7.

[79] The Relations of Banks to Women Entrepreneurs. The Analysis of the Danish Agency for Trade and Industry: Women Entrepreneurs Now and in the Future, Published by the Danish Agency for Trade and Industry, September 2000, available online at http://www.efs.dk/publikationer/rapporter/bankers.uk/index-eng.html. The quotation on single mothers is from part 2.2. The respondents in the analysis were staff in the banks and independant advisors to the banks, eg chartered accountants.

[80] See further McCrudden, Christopher: Equality in Law between Men and Women in the European Community, United Kingdom, Luxembourg 1994 p 15.

7.4. What is sex?

7.4.1. Discrimination against women on grounds of pregnancy and maternity
An analysis of the Danish Agency for Trade and Industry published in 2000 revealed a number of barriers for women entrepreneurs' access to bank loans in the starting phase of a business, see further below in Chapter 4. One of the respondents stated:[81]

'Single mothers do not have much chance of obtaining a loan for their enterprises.'

The respondents in the analysis were staff in the banks and independent advisors to the banks, eg chartered accountants, ie representatives of or advisers to the potential discriminators and not representatives of potential victims. The above statement seems to indicate direct discrimination on grounds of maternity.

7.4.1.1. The proposed Directive on equal treatment in the provision of goods and services
In the Staff Working Paper[82] on the proposed directive on equal treatment in the access to and supply of goods and services refusal to provide a mortgage to pregnant women is mentioned as an example of discrimination which has been brought to the notice of the Commission.

Article 3(a) of the proposed Directive provides that there shall be no direct discrimination based on sex, including less favourable treatment of women for reasons of pregnancy and maternity.

7.4.1.2. Case law of the ECJ
Refusal by an employer to recruit a pregnant woman for an open-ended job because of her pregnancy, and her ensuing incapacity to perform work for a certain period or for health and safety reasons under certain conditions, is according to the practice of the ECJ direct discrimination in violation of the Equal Treatment Directive.

---

[81]   The Relations of Banks to Women Entrepreneurs. The Analysis of the Danish Agency for Trade and Industry: Women Entrepreneurs Now and in the Future, Published by the Danish Agency for Trade and Industry, September 2000, available online at www.efs.dk/publikationer/rapporter/bankers.uk/index-eng.html. The quotation on single mothers is from part 2.2.

[82]   SEC(2003)1213 p 7.

In *Dekker*[83] the ECJ found that an employer is in direct contravention of the principle of equal treatment if he refuses to enter into a contract of employment with a female candidate whom he considers to be suitable for the job where such refusal is based on the possible adverse consequences for him of employing a pregnant woman, owing to rules on unfitness for work adopted by the public authorities.

In the *Gabriele Habermann-Beltermann* v *Arbeiterwohlfahrt, Bezirksverbank Ndb/OpfEV* case[84] the ECJ stated that Article 2(1) and (3), read in conjunction with Articles 3(1) and 5(1) of the Equal Treatment Directive precludes an employment contract without a fixed term for night-time work entered into by an employer and a pregnant employee, both of whom were unaware of the pregnancy, from being held to be void on account of a statutory prohibition on night-time work which applied, by virtue of national law, during pregnancy and breastfeeding, or from being avoided by the employer.

In the case of a contract without a fixed term, the prohibition on night-time work by pregnant women takes effect only for a limited period in relation to the total length of the contract, and to hold the contract invalid or to avoid it because of the temporary inability of the pregnant employee to perform the night-time work for which she was engaged would be contrary to the objective of protecting such persons pursued by Article 2(3) of the directive and would deprive that provision of its effectiveness.

The *Mahlburg*[85] case concerned a nurse who had been refused a permanent post in a Heart Surgery Clinic because she was pregnant. She had been working for the hospital under a fixed-term contract. When a vacancy came up for two permanent posts for operating theatre nurses, she applied. She informed her employers that she was pregnant. As required by German working environment law, for the rest of the period of her fixed term contract the hospital no longer employed her as a nurse in the operating theatre but transferred her to other nursing activities which did not involve a risk of infection. The hospital informed Mahlburg that they had decided not to appoint her to either of the vacant posts. The reason given was the legal requirement which prohibits employers from employing pregnant women in areas where they would be exposed to harmful effects or dangerous substances.

Mahlburg challenged this decision saying that it amounted to discrimination on the grounds of sex. The ECJ agreed. It held that Article 2(1) and (3) of the Equal Treatment Directive precludes a refusal to appoint a pregnant woman to a post for an indefinite period on the ground that a statutory prohibition on employment attaching to the condition of pregnancy prevents her from being employed in that post from the outset and for the duration of the pregnancy.

The above pregnancy cases were all about ordinary, open-ended contracts of employment for an indefinite time. The Danish Supreme Court has submitted questions concerning the applicability of those principles in regard to a fixed

---

[83] Case C-177/88 *Dekker* [1990] ECR I-3941.

[84] Case C-421/92 *Gabriele Habermann-Beltermann* [1994] ECR I-1657.

[85] Case C-207/98, *Mahlburg* [2000] ECR I-549.

term contract in *Tele Danmark*[86] where the economic advantage/disadvantage for the employer, if he is/is not allowed to discriminate on grounds of pregnancy, is greater.

For a number of years it had been a contested issue - both in Danish case law and in doctrinal writing - whether a pregnant woman employed or seeking employment on a time limited contract of such short duration that she, due to her pregnancy, would not be able to work for a significant part of the contracted period is protected against discrimination on grounds of pregnancy by Danish legislation and EU law or whether the employer could argue that overriding economic reasons made it lawful to discriminate.

The case was about a woman, who in June 1995, while she was pregnant, entered into a 6 months employment contract from 1 July 1995 to 31 of December. It was agreed between the parties that she would have to follow a training course during the first two months of her contract. That period was prolonged with two days because of a vacation in connection with her marriage on 12 August. In August 1995, she informed the employer, Tele Danmark that she was pregnant with expected confinement 6 November. Shortly afterwards, on 23 August 1995, she was dismissed with effect from 30 September, ie with the notice she was entitled to under the Danish Salaried Employees Act, on the ground that she had not informed Tele Danmark that she was pregnant when she was recruited. Under the applicable collective agreement, she would have been entitled, had she so wished, to paid maternity leave starting eight weeks before the expected date of birth, ie on 11 September 1995. Tele Danmark argued that the prohibition under Community law of dismissing a pregnant worker did not apply to a worker, recruited on a temporary basis, who, despite knowing that she was pregnant when the contract of employment was concluded, failed to inform the employer of this, and because of her right to maternity leave was unable, for a substantial part of the duration of that contract, to perform the work for which she had been recruited.

The ECJ concluded, in accordance with the proposal by the Advocate General, that Article 5(1) of the Equal Treatment Directive and/or Article 10 of the pregnancy Directive are to be interpreted as precluding a worker from being dismissed on the ground of pregnancy where she was recruited for a fixed period, and she failed to inform the employer that she was pregnant even though she was aware of this when the contract of employment was concluded, and because of her pregnancy she was unable to work during a substantial part of the term of that contract.

---

[86] Case C-109/2000, *Tele Danmark* [2001] ECR I -6993.

The judgment in *Tele Danmark* seems to suggest that economic considerations cannot override the prohibition against discrimination on grounds of pregnancy.

7.4.2. Discrimination on grounds of marital status
In K B[87], the ECJ stated that the fact that certain benefits are restricted to married couples cannot be regarded *per se* as discrimination on grounds of sex.

7.4.3. Discrimination on grounds of sexual orientation
In the *Grant* case,[88] the ECJ concluded that the refusal by an employer to allow travel concessions to the person of the same sex with whom a worker has a stable relationship, where such concessions are allowed to a worker's spouse or to the person of the opposite sex with whom a worker has a stable relationship outside marriage, *does not* constitute discrimination prohibited by Article 141 EC or the Equal Pay Directive.

Discrimination against homosexuals in the provision of goods and services will therefore not be covered by the ban on discrimination in the proposed Directive.

7.5. Separate but equal treatment

Article 1(3) of the proposed Directive on equal treatment in the provision of goods and services provides that the Directive does not preclude differences which are related to goods or services for which men and women are not in a comparable situation because the goods or services are intended exclusively or primarily for the members of one sex or to skills which are practised differently for each sex. In the explanatory remarks[89] it is explained that certain goods and services are specifically designed for use by members of one sex (for example, single-sex sessions in a swimming pool). The provision is discussed further below in Chapter 4 under market segmentation by gender.

The Danish Complaints Board for Equality has held that it was not a violation of the ban on sex discrimination in the Danish Equal Status Act that an organisation (Hitzb-ut-tahrir) provided access to a public meeting through separate entrances of equal quality for men and women.[90]

---

[87] Case C-117/01, *K B* [2004] ECR I-0000 (nyr, judgment of 7 January 2004).

[88] Case C-249/96 *Lisa Jacqueline Grant* v *South-West Trains Ltd* ECR [1998] I-0621.

[89] COM(2003)756 p 13.

[90] The decision is available (in Danish) at www.ligenaevn.dk.

7.6. No defence against direct discrimination

The orthodox view in EU law is that (except for derogations from the ban on sex discrimination) there is[91] no defence that can justify direct discrimination. It can, for example, not be justified by reference to the fact that the discriminator will incur considerable costs if he does not discriminate.

In *Dekker*[92] the distinction between direct and indirect sex discrimination was at issue. In this case an employer refused to engage a woman because she was three months pregnant and the employer's insurer would not reimburse the maternity payments payable during the maternity leave. The Hoge Raad (the Dutch Supreme Court) referred questions to the ECJ as to whether an employer infringes, directly or indirectly, the principle of equal treatment if he refuses to enter into a contract of employment with a suitable applicant *on the ground that the applicant's pregnancy*, existent at the time of the application, *might have adverse financial effects* for the employer due to provisions in national law. The Hoge Raad also asked whether it makes any diference whether there were male applicants.

The ECJ observed that only women can be refused employment on grounds of pregnancy and such a refusal therefore constitutes direct discrimination on grounds of sex. A refusal of employment on account of the financial consequences of absence due to pregnancy must be regarded as based, essentially, on the fact of pregnancy . Such discrimination cannot be justified on grounds relating to the financial loss which an employer who appointed a pregnant woman would suffer for the duration of her maternity leave.

The question whether direct discrimination may sometimes be justified, for example on grounds of serious economic costs of gender equality, is, however, contested. In *Birds Eye Wall*[93] the Commission and Advocate General thus argued that economic justification should be possible, see also below in chapter 4 on the use of actuarial factors in pensions.

---

[91] See for a fuller discussion on this point Lynn M. Roseberry: The Limits of Employment Discrimination Law in the United States and European Community, Copenhagen 1999 p 77 et seq.

[92] Case C-177/88, *Dekker* ECR [1990] I-3941.

[93] Case C-132/ 91, *Birds Eye Walls* [1993] ECR I-5579.

8. Indirect Sex Discrimination

The current definition of indirect discrimination is inspired by the case law of the ECJ in cases involving the free movement of workers.[94]

8.1. Historical development of the definition of indirect discrimination

8.1.1. The UK as forerunner in the definition of indirect sex discrimination
Section 1(1) of the UK Sex Discrimination Act (SDA)1975 defines indirect discrimination against women for the purposes of inter alia the provision of goods and services. In any circumstances relevant for the purposes of any provision of the SDA outside of the employment field a person discriminates against a woman if:

> 1(1)(b) he applies to her a requirement or condition which he applies or would apply equally to a man but:
> 1(1)(b)(i) which is such that the proportion of women who can comply with it is considerably smaller than the proportion of men who can comply with it, and
> 1(1)(b)(ii) which he cannot show to be justifiable irrespective of the sex of the person to whom it is applied, and
> 1(1)(b)(iii) which is to her detriment because she cannot comply with it.

The above provision is to be read as applying equally to the treatment of men, and for that purpose shall have effect with such modifications as are requisite. In the application of this provision no account shall be taken of special treatment afforded to women in connection with pregnancy or childbirth.

8.1.2. EU law
Until the adoption of the Burden of Proof Directive in 1997[95] EU legislation contained no definition of what constitutes indirect discrimination on grounds of sex. The Equal Treatment Directive 1976[96] and the Equal Treatment in Social Security Directive 1979[97] referred to indirect discrimination but did not provide a definition of the concept.

---

[94] See in particular Case C-237/ 94, *O'Flynn* [1996] ECR 2417.

[95] 97/80/EC.

[96] 76/207/EEC Article 2(1).

[97] 79/7/EEC Article 4(1).

8.1.2.1. The case-law of the ECJ[98]

A number of criteria are often gender related depending on the social context. Some criteria may be gender related in one EU country and not in another. The part-time criterion has been widely used in national labour and social legislation and employment practice. On a number of occasions, the ECJ has held that differential treatment of full time and part time workers constitutes indirect discrimination on grounds of sex because a considerably larger proportion of women than men work part-time.

In *Jenkins* v *Kingsdale*,[99] the ECJ was for the first time presented with the problem whether different hourly rates for full time and part time workers constitute a breach of Community provisions on equal pay. The ruling of the Court did not lay down that discrimination between part-time and full-time workers *per se* constitutes indirect discrimination on grounds of sex. It only regarded a difference in pay between part-time and full-time workers as a breach of Article 141 EC if it is in reality an indirect way of reducing women's pay (because most part-time workers are women). Whether this is the case must be decided by the national courts.

In *Ingrid Rinner-Kühn*[100] a German court put the question as to whether Article 141 EC was breached if national legislation laid down that only employees working more than 10 hours per week were entitled to sick pay from the employer, and if significantly more women than men were employed for less than 10 hours per week. The ECJ held in the operative part of the judgment that Article 141 EC must be interpreted as precluding national legislation which permits employers to exclude employees whose normal working hours do not exceed 10 hours a week or 45 hours a month from the continued payment of wages in the event of illness, if that measure affects a far greater number of women than men, unless the Member State shows that the legislation concerned is justified by objective factors unrelated to any discrimination on grounds of sex.

In *Bilka*,[101] the ECJ found that if, a much lower proportion of women than of men work full time, the exclusion of part-time workers from an occupational pension scheme would be contrary to Article 141 EC where, taking into account the difficulties encountered by women workers in working full-time, that measure could not be explained by factors which exclude any discrimination on

---

[98]   O'Leary, Siofra: Employment Law at the European Court of Justice. Judicial Structures, Policies and Processes, London 2002 p 141*et seq.*

[99]   Case 96/80, *Jenkins* [1981] ECR 911.

[100]   Case C-171/88, *Rinner-Kühn* [1989] ECR 2743.

[101]   Case 170/84, *Bilka* [1986] ECR 1607.

grounds of sex. However, if the undertaking was able to show that its pay practice may be explained by objectively justified factors unrelated to any discrimination on grounds of sex there was no breach of Article 141 EC.

8.1.2.2. The definition in the Burden of Proof Directive

Article2(2) of the Burden of Proof Directive 1997 defines the concept of indirect discrimination on grounds of sex in the following way (emphasis added):

> ... indirect discrimination shall exist where an apparently neutral provision, criterion or practice *disadvantages* a *substantially higher proportion* of the members of one sex unless that provision, criterion or practice isappropriate and necessary and can be justified by objective factors unrelated to sex.

8.1.2.3. The definition in the Article 13 Directives from 2000, the amended Equal Treatment Directive from 2002 and the proposed directive on equal treatment in the provision of goods and services from 2003

The Article 13 Directives from 2000[102] and the amended Equal Treatment Directive from 2002[103] define indirect discrimination in a similar way, namely as (emphasis added):

> (b) indirect discrimination: where an apparently neutral provision, criterion or practice *would put* persons of one sex *at a particular disadvantage* compared with persons of the other sex, unless that provision, criterion or practice is objectively justified by a legitimate aim, and the means of achieving that aim are appropriate and necessary.

The Proposal for a Directive on Equal Treatment in the Provision of Goods and Services from 2003 defines indirect discrimination in the same way as the amended Equal Treatment Directive from 2002. The English versions of the two provisions are identical, see further below.

According to this definition, an apparently neutral provision, criterion or practice will be regarded as indirectly discriminatory if it is intrinsically liable to adversely affect a person or persons on the grounds referred to in the Directive. This 'liability test' may be proven on the basis of statistical evidence or by any other means that demonstrate that a provision would be intrinsically

---

[102] 2000/43/EC on race discrimination which in addition to employmentapplies *inter alia* to contracts for the provision of goods and services and the employment framework directivve 2000/78/EC on discrimination on grounds of religion, age, handicap and sexual orientation.

[103] 2002/73/EC.

disadvantageous for the person or persons concerned. This definition is modelled over the jurisprudence of the ECJ in the *O'Flynn*[104] case.

In the explanatory memorandum to the proposal for a Directive on equal treatment in the provision of goods and services the Commission states that the definitions are drawn from existing Community law and do not depart from previously agreed approaches in any way. The concepts of direct and indirect discrimination and sex-based and sexual harassment are, *mutatis mutandis*, identical to those contained in the already Article 13 Directives from 2000[105] and the amended Equal Treatment Directive from 2002[106]

8.2. Apparently neutral provision, criterion or practice. Suspect criteria

A number of criteria are gender related depending on the social context. The part-time criterion has been widely used in national labour and social legislation and employment practice. In the Staff Working Paper[107] on the proposed directive on equal treatment in the access to and supply of goods and services refusal to offer loans to people working part-time is mentioned asan example of existing discriminatory practice.

On a number of occasions, the ECJ has held that differential treatment of full time and part time workers constitutes indirect discrimination on grounds of sex because a considerably larger proportion of women than men work part-time,[108] see for example *Rinner-Kühn,*[109] *Jenkins*[110] and *Bilka.*[111]

---

[104]   Case C-237/94, *O'Flynn* [1996] ECR I-2617.

[105]   2000/43/EC on race discrimination which in addition to employment applies *inter alia* to contracts for the provision of goods and services and the employment framework directivve 2000/78/EC on discrimination on grounds of religion, age, handicap and sexual orientation.

[106]   2002/73/EC.

[107]   SEC(2003)1213 p 7.

[108]   See for more detail Nielsen, Ruth: European Labour Law, Copenhagen 2000 Chapter V.

[109]   Case C-171/88, *Rinner-Kühn* [1989] ECR 2743.

[110]   Case 96/80, *Jenkins* [1981] ECR 911.

[111]   Case 170/84, *Bilka* [1986] ECR 1607.

8.3. Would put members of one sex at a particular disadvantage

The Proposal for a Directive on Equal Treatment in the Provision of Goods and Services from 2003 defines indirect discrimination in the same way as the amended Equal Treatment Directive from 2002. The English versions of the two provisions are identical, whereas there are minor differences in the wording in other language versions.

As the definition of indirect discrimination is worded[112] in the proposed Directive it is not necessary for there to be indirect discrimination that a formally neutral criterion actually operates to the disadvantage of one sex. It is sufficient that there is a possibility that the criterion would put one sex at a disadvantage.

Before 2000, the definition of indirect discrimination required disparate effect, ie that a colnsiderable higher percentage of one sex than of the other should be affected by the apparently neutral meaure. In the Race Discrimination Directive[113] the wording was changed so that what is decisive is that the contested criterion would put members of one sex at a particular disadvantage. This may be proven on the basis of statistical evidence or by any other means that demonstrate that a provision would be intrinsically disadvantageous for the person or persons concerned. This definition is modelled over the jurisprudence of the ECJ in the *O'Flynn*[114] case.

8.4. Objectively justified

Indirect discrimination may be justified by objective reasons. The starting point is that differential treatment is an expression of discrimination unless it can be shown that such treatment is justified in objective terms.

The leading case is still *Bilka*[115] where the ECJ ruled that Article 141 EC is infringed by an undertaking which excludes part-time employees from its occupational pension scheme, where that exclusion affects a far greater number of women than men, unless the undertaking shows that the exclusion is based on *objectively justified factors unrelated to any discrimination* on grounds of sex. Such factors may lie in the fact that the undertaking seeks to employ as few

---

[112] The English version reads: 'would put at a disadvantage', the French version: 'est susceptible d'entraîner un désavantage' and the German version: 'können benachteiligen'.

[113] 2000/43/EC.

[114] Case C-237/94, *O'Flynn* [1996] ECR I-2617.

[115] Case 170/84, *Bilka* [1986] ECR 1607.

part-time workers as possible, where it is shown that that objective corresponds to a *real need* on the part of the undertaking and the means chosen for achieving it are *appropriate* and *necessary*. The ECJ thus requires three conditions to be met:

1) There must be a real need for the employer to apply the "suspect" criteria,
2) the means chosen by the employer must be necessary to achieve this goal, and
3) the means must be appropriate, ie there must be a reasonable proportion between end and means.

The *Bilka* test is based on application of the *principle of proportionality*.

8.4.1. Legitimate aim unrelated to any discrimination based on sex

8.4.1.1. Market factors. Commercial aims

In *Enderby*,[116] the ECJ stated that it is for the national jurisdiction to decide, applying if necessary the principle of proportionality, if, and in what measure, the shortage of candidates for a particular post and the necessity of attracting them by a higher salary constitutes an objective economic reason justifying the difference in remuneration between the two tasks in issue.

In *Enderby* the ECJ used a wording which seems to accept economic grounds as legitimate aims which may be unrelated to any discrimination related to sex.. It stated:

25. The Court has consistently held that it is for the national court, which has sole jurisdiction to make findings of fact, to determine whether and to what extent the grounds put forward by an employer to explain the adoption of a pay practice which applies independently of a worker's sex but in fact affects more women than men may be regarded as objectively justified economic grounds (Case 170/84 Bilka-Kaufhaus, cited above, at paragraph 36 and Case C-184/89 Nimz, cited above, at paragraph 14). Those grounds may include, if they can be attributed to the needs and objectives of the undertaking, different criteria such as the worker's flexibility or adaptability to hours and places of work, his training or his length of service (Case 109/88 Danfoss, cited above, at paragraphs 22 to 24).

---

[116]   Case C-127/ 92, *Enderby* [1993] ECR I-5535.

The ECJ also showed some acceptance of economic reasons as justification in *Jämställdhetsombudsmannen.*[117]

8.4.1.2. Budgetary considerations

In *Schönheit*,[118] the ECJ confirmed its case law to the effect that restricting public expenditure is not an objective which may be relied on to justify different treatment on grounds of sex. It stated:

> The Court has already held that budgetary considerations cannot justify discrimination against one of the sexes. To concede that such considerations may justify a difference in treatment between men and women which would otherwise constitute indirect discrimination on grounds of sex would mean that the application and scope of a rule of Community law as fundamental as that of equal treatment between men and women might vary in time and place according to the state of the public finances of Member States (Roks, paragraphs 35 and 36; Case C-226/98 Jørgensen [2000] ECR I-2447, paragraph 39; and Kutz-Bauer, paragraphs 59 and 60).

The different treatment of men and women may be justified, depending on the circumstances, by reasons other than those put forward at the time when the measure introducing the difference in treatment was introduced. In *Roks*,[119] the ECJ stated:

> 36. Moreover, to concede that budgetary considerations may justify a difference in treatment as between men and women which would otherwise constitute indirect discrimination on grounds of sex, which is prohibited by Article 4(1) of Directive 79/7, would be to accept that the application and scope of as fundamental a rule of Community law as that of equal treatment between men and women might vary in time and place according to the state of the public finances of the Member States.

8.4.1.3. When must the legitimate aims be disclosed?

In *Schönheit*,[120] the ECJ stated that different treatment of men and women, which in that case arose from legislation, may be justified, depending on the circumstances, by reasons other than those put forward at the time when the legislation introducing the difference in treatment was introduced.

---

[117]   Case C-236/98 *Jämställdhetsombudsmannen* [2000] ECR I-2189.

[118]   Joined Cases C-4/02 and C-5/02 *Schönheit* [2003] ECR 0000 (nyr).

[119]   Case C-343/92 *M A De Weerd, née Roks* [1994] ECR I-571.

[120]   Joined Cases C-4/02 and C-5/02, *Schönheit* [2003] ECR 0000 (nyr).

8.4.2. Means

The means used to achieve the legitimate aim must be appropriate and necessary. If other means that are unrelated to sex could have been used, the justification test fails. The means must no be excessive. The general principle they are to be measured by is, as mentioned, the principle of proportionality.

8.4.3. Conclusion. Can the justification test be passed by reference to commercial considerations?

The lessons that can be learned from the practice on indirect sex discrimination in empl oyment cases are unclear. The ECJ has often been criticised for inconsistencies in its case law on this issue.[121] It is, however, settled case law that general assertions are not enough to satisfy the requirements for justification. In *Seymour-Smith and Perez*,[122] the ECJ thus held that mere generalisations concerning the capacity of a specific measure to encourage recruitment are not enough to show that the aim of the disputed rule is unrelated to any discrimination based on sex nor to provide evidence on the basis of which it could reasonably be considered that the means chosen were suitable for achieving that aim.

In comparison it may be mentioned that in January 2004, the Commission presented a draft proposal for a Directive on Services which contains a ban on discrimination on grounds of nationality.[123] Article 21 of the proposed directive provides:

> 'Non-discrimination. 1. Member States shall ensure that the recipient is not subjected to discriminatory requirements based on his nationality or place of residence.'

In the explanatory memorandum it is stated that the principle of non-discrimination in the Internal Market implies that access by recipients - particularly consumers - to services offered to the public should not be denied or rendered more difficult simply because of the formal criterion of the recipient's nationality or place of residence. Consequently, the Directive lays down, obligations for Member States and service-providers. For service providers, the proposal in Article 21(2) prohibits them, in their general conditions relating to access to their services, from providing for refusal of access, or subjecting

---

[121]   See further O'Leary, Siofra: Employment Law at the European Court of Justice. Judicial Structures, Policies and Processes, London 2002.

[122]   Case C-167/97, *Seymour-Smith* [1999] ECR I-623.

[123]   europa.eu.int/comm/internal_market/en/services/services/ docs/2004-proposal_en. pdf. It is provisional and subject to further linguistic revisions.

access to less favourable conditions, on grounds of the nationality or place of residence of the recipient.

This does not prevent service providers from refusing to provide services or applying different tariffs and conditions *if they can demonstrate that this is directly justified by objective reasons*, such as actual additional costs resulting from the distances involved or the technical aspects of the service.

The above proposal for a directive on services is mainly motivated by a desire to ensure the smooth functioning of the internal market. In matters of gender equality where there is a strong fundamental rights perspective the justification test of economic reasons will probably be stricter.

8.5. Link between gender mainstreaming and indirect sex discrimination

The mainstreaming principle applies both at EU level and Member State level. If a Member State retains legislation with adverse gender impact it is violating the mainstreaming policy endorsed by Article 3(2) EC. It may also be violating the ban against indirect sex discrimination.

The conceptual links between 'mainstreaming' and 'indirect discrimination' are, however, only vaguely developed. The words 'mainstreaming' and "indirect discrimination" are seldomly used in the same documents.[124] In the case law of the ECJ the word 'mainstreaming' is not used at all but the mainstreaming provision in Article 3(2) EC has been invoked. In *Dory*[125] AG Stix-Hackl thus argued that there is an obligation for the ECJ to interpret anti-discriminatory Community measures[126] in light of Article 3(2)EC.

Gender impact assessment would appear to be a common element of gender mainstreaming and indirect discrimination. In order to mainstream equality into all areas of society it is necessary to make gender impact assessments of legislation and policy measures.[127] If there is adverse gender impact there may well also be indirect sex discrimination, see above.

---

[124]   See as examples Resolution on the Annual Report from the Commission: Equal opportunities for women and men in the European Union 1996 (COM(96)650 C4-0084/97), OJ C 304 p.45, Opinion of the Economic and Social Committee on 'Equal opportunities for women and men in the European Union - 1996' OJ C 296 p. 24, Resolution on implementation of equal opportunities for men and women in the civil service OJ C 362 p. 337.

[125]   Case C-186/01, *Alexander Dory* v *Deutschland* [2003] ECR I-2479, point 102-3.

[126]   In *Dory* the old Equal Treatment Directive 76/207/EEC.

[127]   Compare the Commission's Guide on Impact Assessment, Brussels 1998.

9. Harassment

The proposed Directive prohibits both harassment and sexual harassment. Harassment (as different from sexual harassment) harassment occurs where unwanted conduct related to the sex of a person is exhibited with the purpose or effect of violating the dignity of a person and of creating an intimidating, hostile, degrading, humiliating or offensive environment. The two concepts of harassment and sexual harassment are defined separately, because they are distinct phenomena. Harassment based on sex consists of unfavourable treatment of a person related to their sex, though it need not be of a sexual nature (an example might be male employee constantly making disparaging remarks about women customers).[128]

10. Sexual Harassment

Sexual harassment is unwelcome physical, verbal or non-verbal conduct of a sexual nature. Sexual harassment can include: comments about the way the person looks, indecent remarks, questions or comments about the person's sex life, requests for sexual favours, sexual demands and any conduct of a sexual nature which creates an intimidating, hostile or humiliating environment.

It is most often women who are subjected to sexual harassment, but men too can be sexually harassed.

Under English law harassment of a client or customer by a member of staff is unlawful under the SDA and the organisation can find itself facing a legal challenge under section 41 SDA.[129] In its Good practice guide: service

---

[128]   COM(2003)756 p 13.

[129]   SDA section 41(1) provides: Anything done by a person in the course of his employment shall be treated for the purposes of this Act as done by his employer as well as by him, whether or not it was done with the employer's knowledge or approval. SDA section 41(3) provides: 41(3) In proceedings brought under this Act against any person in respect of an act alleged to have been done by an employee of his it shall be a defence for that person to prove that he took such steps as were reasonably practicable to prevent the employee from doing that act, or from doing in the course of his employment acts of that description. SDA section 42(1) provides: A person who knowingly aids another person to do an act made unlawful by this Act shall be treated for the purposes of this Act as himself doing an unlawful act of the like description. SDA section 42(1) provides: For the purposes of subsection (1) an employee or agent for whose act the employer or principal is liable under section 41 (or would be so liable but for section 41(3)) shall be deemed to aid the doing of the act by the employer or principal.

delivery,[130] the EOC mentions the following case as an example of unlawful sexual harassment in the provision of a service (driving lessons):

> A woman alleged that her driving instructor had sexually harassed her during driving lessons by making comments of a sexual nature and staring at her legs. She took proceedings in Belfast County Court against the driving instructor and the driving school. She claimed that her instructor was not providing her with facilities or services 'in the like manner' as would be provided to a man. The court found that the instructor's behaviour amounted to sex discrimination as he would not have treated a male pupil in the same way. The driving school was also found liable as they had failed to take reasonable steps to prevent the instructor from discriminating against the woman.

11. Incitements to Discriminate

According to Article 2(2) of the proposed Directive incitement to direct or indirect discrimination on grounds of sex shall be deemed to be discrimination within the meaning of the Directive.

12. Victimisation

Article 9 of the proposed Directive on equal treatment in the access to and supply of goods and services provides:

> Member States shall introduce into their national legal systems such measures as are necessary to protect persons from any adverse treatment or adverse consequence as a reaction to a complaint or to legal proceedings aimed at enforcing compliance with the principle of equal treatment.

This provision builds on the case law of the ECJ in the *Coote*,[131] see below in Chapter 5. Protection against victimisation is increasingly provided for in EU discrimination law. This provision in the proposed Directive will require changes in most of the existing national equality acts.

---

[130]   available at www.eoc.org.uk.

[131]   Case C-185/97 *Belinda Jane Coote* v *Granada Hospitality Ltd* [1998] ECR I-5199.

Chapter 4

Formation, Validity, Content and Performance

1. Introduction

In this chapter I discuss whether there is freedom to, a duty to, or a prohibition against taking gender into account when preparing and making decisions on the formation, validity, content and performance of contracts for the provision of goods and services.

2. The concept of contract

2.1. The traditional view

Traditionally there is deemed to be a contract when a promise has been accepted by the person it is addressed to. A contractual relationship is made up of a number of interacting statements of intention (offer, acceptance, etc).

In legal writing partly opposing theories: the Will-theory, the Expectation theory and the Declaration theory have traditionally been discussed. Under classical contract law (ie contract law as developed around the turn from the 19th to the 20th century) freedom of contract was seen as the fundamental principle. A contract was seen as founded upon the will of the parties and considered binding for the parties, primarily because it reflected the intention of the parties, either the intention of the promisor to be bound by the promise as an expression of his will, or the intention of the relying party to be bound by what he could reasonably expect.

In modern contract law it is not only the will or reliance of the parties which is decisive when dealing with contract law issues such as formation of contract, interpretation of contracts and the effects of breach of contract but also party external criteria, for example the need to protect the weaker party or - as discussed in this book - the fundamental right and general principle of gender equality. It is often stressed that there is a shift in focus from subjective to more objective aspects of the contractual setting.[1]

---

[1]   See further Ulfbeck, Vibe: Kontrakters relativitet, Copenhagen 2000.

2.2. EU law

During the last 30 years the concept of a contract is increasingly being shaped and re-shaped by EU law. A number of EU provisions on contracts define the specific kind of contract governed by the specific piece of legislation. As examples the Directives on public procurement,[2] the Directive on consumer credit[3] and the time share Directive[4] may be mentioned. EU law also uses the concepts of standard contracts[5] and distance contracts.[6]

In the Commission's Communication a more Coherent European Contract Law. An Action Plan[7] from February 2003, the Commission states that future proposals for contract law provisions will, where appropriate, take into account a common frame of reference, which the Commission intends to elaborate via research and with the help of all interested parties. This common frame of reference should provide for best solutions in terms of common terminology and rules, ie the definition of fundamental concepts and abstract terms like 'contract'.

2.3. The proposed Directive on equal treatment in the provision of goods and services

In the proposal for a Directive on equal treatment in the provision of goods and services[8] the term 'contract' is not used in the title of the Directive which also does not offer a definition of the concepts of a contract and only makes scant use of the word contract.

---

[2] 92/50/EEC, 93/36/EEC and 93/37/EEC as amended by 97/52/EC. A new procurement directive was adopted in February 2004 and is at the time of writing awaiting publication in the Official Journal.

[3] 87/102/EEC with later amendments.

[4] 94/47/EC.

[5] 93/13/EEC on unfair terms in consumer contracts.

[6] 97/7/EC on consumer protection in respect of distance contracts and 2002/65/EC concerning the distance marketing of consumer financial services.

[7] COM(2003)68.

[8] COM(2003)756.

In the preamble[9] it is stated that the use of actuarial factors related to sex should be eliminated. To avoid a sudden readjustment of the market, the prohibition of the use of such factors should apply only to new *contracts* concluded after the date of transposition of the Directive and should be phased in over a sufficiently long period. The Directive should not therefore apply to the use of such factors in *contracts* concluded for the first time before that date.

Article 4 of the proposed directive provides that Member States shall ensure that the use of sex as a factor in the calculation of premiums and benefits for the purpose of insurance and related financial services is prohibited in all new *contracts*.

Article 12 on compliance provides that any provisions contrary to the principle of equal treatment included in individual or collective *contracts* or agreements, internal rules of undertakings, and rules governing profit making or non-profit-making associations are, or may be declared, null and void or are amended.

Article 12 is a standard provision in discrimination directives. In respect of the Equal Treatment Directive,[10] the ECJ held in *Commission* v *UK*[11] that the directive covers all collective agreements (which typically are not binding contracts under UK law) without distinction as to the nature of the legal effects which they do or do not produce. The reason for that generality lies in the fact that, even if they are not legally binding as between the parties who sign them or with regard to the employment relationships which they govern, collective agreements nevertheless have important de facto consequences for the employment relationships to which they refer, particularly in so far as they determine the rights of the workers and, in the interests of industrial harmony, give undertakings some indication of the conditions which employment relationships must satisfy or need not satisfy. The need to ensure that the directive is completely effective therefore requires that any clauses in such agreements which are incompatible with the obligations imposed by the directive upon the member states may be rendered inoperative, eliminated or amended by appropriate means.

The null and void remedy thus applies to a broad range of statements irrespective of whether they are contracts in a strict sense.

The word 'contract' is only used twice in the explanatory remarks, namely in the following contexts:

---

[9] Recital 13.

[10] 76/207/EEC.

[11] Case 165/82, *Commission* v *United Kingdom* [1983] ECR 3431.

As the European Court of Justice made clear in the Defrenne II case13, the proper implementation of equal treatment requires not only that the law should conform to the principle but that rules found in collective agreements and private contracts should also be brought into line.[12]

Harassment on grounds of sex and sexual harassment do not occur solely in the workplace, but can also occur in other areas... Examples in this area might include harassment... by company buyers of salespeople, where, for example, sexual favours may be demanded in return for the award of contracts.[13]

In the Commission Staff Working Paper underlying the proposal the word contract is used ten times.[14]

2.4. The whole contracting process

In this book, the concept of contract law is used in a broad sense. I look at the whole contracting process from commercial communications made with a view to establishing contractual links to the solution of conflicts arising in connection with contractual arrangements. In the communication[15] from 2001 with which the Commission launched the current debate on European contract law it also used a broad concept of contract law covering eg product liability and data protection. Product liability is not discussed in the present book but data protection is, in my view, an important issue both in contract law and discrimination law and is discussed in more detail below in section 10.

2.5. Contract law and tort law

There is a blurred borderline between contract law and tort law with regard to discrimination. In academic writing, harassment and sexual harassment have until now more often been discussed as a matter of tort law[16] than of contract law. The pending proposal for a directive on equal treatment in the provision of goods and

---

[12] COM(2003)756 p 8.

[13] Op cit p 13.

[14] See SEC(2003)1213 p 8, 10, 18 and 19.

[15] COM(2001)98.

[16] See for example Conaghan, Joanne and Wade Mansell: The wrongs of tort, London 1999, in particular Chapter 7 on Feminist Perspectives on Tort Law: Remedying Sexual Harassment and Abuse.

services prohibits harassment and sexual harassment in contracting and thus cuts across traditional distinctions between contract law and tort law.

2.6. Commercial contracts and consumer contracts

Gender equality is a problem both as regards consumer contracts and commercial contracts. Most consumer decisions are probably made by women[17] and in that sense consumer law is women's law. Women are often buyers in contracts for the provision of goods and services used by men and children of either sex.

The parallel between discrimination in employment and discrimination in business is probably most notable in respect of commercial contracts. Women-led businesses and women-owned businesses will often encounter some of the same kinds of discrimination as those which women experience when mounting the career-ladder in employment, for example in connection with raising capital and obtaining commercial loans.

3. Market Segmentation by Gender

In the following I discuss whether market segmentation by gender constitutes direct or indirect discrimination within the meaning of gender equality law.

3.1. Gender-based market segmentation as a business practice

Gender is a very commonly used basis for segmenting markets. Not only does it often correspond to differences in buying behaviour, it is also an easy one to measure. Firms can have a reasonably good idea of the *gender* specific market in a given area from a variety of sources. Gender profiling on the basis of processing of personal data collected during the contracting process is discussed further below in section 10.

The gender dimension is also well integrated in higher education in marketing. While it is possible to pass a law degree in most European universities without knowing the basics of gender equality law it is hardly possible to pass a degree in marketing at a European business school without having learned

---

[17] Se for example Quinlan, Mary Lou: Just Ask a Woman - cracking the code of what women want and how they buy, New York 2003 p 1 who estimates that 85% of consumer decisions in consumer sales are made by women. See also www.ewowfacts.com.

119

something about market segmentation by gender - both its advantages and disadvantages for business.[18]

The underlying principle of the market-segmentation process is that similar customers are grouped together. The process is generally considered to consist of three stages: segmentation, targeting, and positioning. Blois and Dibb describe the segmentation process in the following way:[19]

> During the segmentation stage, customers are grouped into segments using one or a combination of variables. The aim is to collect together those with similar needs and buying behaviour. For example, the market for magazines can be segmented using the *gender* and age of consumers. There are titles targeting pre-school children, teenage girls, 20 - 35 year old males, and the over 50s. Next, marketers choose the segment(s) on which to target marketing resources. The final stage, positioning, involves the design of marketing programmes that will match the requirements of customers in the segments chosen. The marketing programmes should position the product or service directly at the targeted customers.

With the increase in e-commerce the possibilities for collecting gender related information and building user profiles broken down by gender have increased considerably. Data enabling a seller to target groups and individuals by gender are collected as a matter of routine in e-business, see for example the following citation (emphasis added):[20]

> With a profile tool, site owners typically use a registration form or transaction to ask users for demographic (eg age, income, education, *gender*, etc.) .. Because personalization products also have tracking components, the Web publisher can associate clickstreams with individual user profiles or groups of people based on a single profile characteristic (eg *gender*, favourite type of movie, profession, *marital status*, and more). Building user profiles helps marketers determine patterns and trends among customers, in whole or in segments.

There are also businesses who make a living of advising on how to sell to a specific gender group, for example women.[21] The above business practices may

---

[18] See for example Palmer, Adrian: Principles of Marketing, Oxford 2000.

[19] Cf Blois, Keith and Sally Dibb: The Oxford Textbook of Marketing, Oxford 2000.

[20] Allen, Cliff, Deborah Kania and Beth Yaeckel: One-to-One Web Marketing: Build a Relationship. Marketing Strategy. One Customer at a Time, New York 2002 p 123. The lawfulness or otherwise under data protection law of gender-profiling is discussed further below in Chapter 4.

[21] The book Quinlan, Mary Lou: Just Ask a Woman - cracking the code of what women want and how they buy, New York 2003 is, for example, presented by the publisher

result both in isolated instances of sex discrimination and in more sustained discriminatory practices.

In marketing literature there are, as mentioned in Chapter 3, warnings against confusing the use of *gender* as a basis for market segmentation with a classification based on biological sex. Many marketers have moved on from segmentation based on a dichotomous male/female classification to a segmentation basis which recognizes a wide range of *gender* orientations. For example, the lifestyle and buying behaviour of career women is likely to be different from that of housewives.[22]

3.2. Goods and services specifically designed for members of one sex

In the proposal for a Directive on equal treatment in the provision of goods and services Article 1(3) provides:

> 3. This Directive does not preclude differences which are related to goods or services for which men and women are not in a comparable situation because the goods or services are intended exclusively or primarily for the members of one sex or to skills which are practised differently for each sex.

The Preamble[23] contains a similar statement. In the explanatory remarks[24] it is explained that certain goods and services are specifically designed for use by members of one sex (for example, single-sex sessions in a swimming pool or private membership clubs). In other cases, the same skills may be practised differently depending on whether the customer is a man or a woman. The directive should not interfere with such differences, where men and women are not in a comparable situation. To avoid inappropriate interpretations of the prohibition of discrimination, the article makes clear that the directive does not preclude differences of treatment when they are based on goods or services which are intended exclusively or primarily for members of one sex or the other or on skills which are practised differently for one sex or the other.

One should , however, be careful not to confuse the user and the buyer of goods and services. Women are buyers of many products and services which are

---

as 'a guide for marketers, advertisers and brand managers ... written by the founder of a consultancy dedicated to marketing to women...'.

[22] Palmer, Adrian: Principles of Marketing, Oxford 2000 p 59.

[23] Recital 12.

[24] COM(2003)756 p 13.

used by men or children of either sex. In literature[25] on market segmentation by gender it is for example stated:

> We do, however, need to be careful how we use *gender* as a basis for market segmentation. Firstly, it has to be remembered that one of the criteria for effective segmentation is that it should identify homogeneity in buying behaviour. There is a lot of evidence that, for many products, a person of one *gender* may buy a product which is intended for use by another *gender*. It has been estimated in the UK, for example that over half of all men's underwear is purchased by women, with men having a relatively minor part in the buying process. The segment of men's underwear buyers which should be of interest to manufacturers should therefore be women. The way that women buy underwear, the retailers that they buy from, and the features that they look for are likely to be quite different from the processes of men and the features that they look for. It follows therefore that the female buyer segment represents an important segment for manufacturers of men's underwear.

The fact that men's underwear is designed specifically for men is no reason for allowing female buyers of men's underwear to be treated differently from male buyers.

In respect of personal services it may be different. Gentlemen's hairdressers are, for example, probably allowed to limit their services to members of the male sex. If a hairdresser offers services to both sexes similar services cannot lawfully be offered at different prices, see also above in Chapter 3 on separate but equal treatment.

4. Capacity to Contract

As set out in Chapter 2, CEDAW Article 15 provides that States Parties shall accord to women, in civil matters, a legal capacity identical to that of men and the same opportunities to exercise that capacity. In particular, they shall give women equal rights to conclude contracts.

In pre-industrial societies direct, formal discrimination between men's and women's capacity to contract was/is usual typically resulting in women - or subgroups of women, eg married women - being barred from contracting.

4.1. Formal capacity to contract

In Europe such direct, overt, formal discrimination in the capacity to contract was abolished in the late 19th and early 20th century. In the proposal from 2003 for a Directive on equal treatment between women and men in the access to and

---

[25] Segmentation and Targeting By: Palmer, Adrian: Principles of Marketing, Oxford 2000 p 59.

supply of goods and services and the underlying Staff Working Paper[26] this kind of discrimination is not explicitly discussed probably because it is supposed to be too 'old-fashioned' to be of relevance in an EU context. The problems women encounter in obtaining equity capital and credit facilities consist, however, often in a mixture of direct and indirect discrimination.

4.2. Equal opportunities to exercise the capacity to contract

CEDAW Article 15 not only requires identical legal capacity to contract for men and women but also that men and women shall enjoy the same opportunities to exercise that capacity. In that respect there are still considerable problems, particularly in financial services and the agricultural sector where there are gender gaps in market access and market structures. The proposal from 2003 for a Directive on equal treatment in the provision of goods and services identified the financial services sector as a particularly problematic area.

With regard to self-employed workers, ie all persons pursuing a gainful activity for their own account including farmers and members of the liberal professions and their spouses there is a Directive from 1986 on equal treatment which requires the absence of all discrimination on grounds of sex, either directly or indirectly, by reference in particular to marital or family status.[27] It may be argued that all gender related hindrances to women's businesses, eg discriminatory practices in entering investment or credit contracts, are contrary to that directive but so far - nearly 15 years after the dead-line for implementing the directive - some problems remain more or less the same as they have been for a number of years.

4.2.1. Access to own land (agricultural holdings)

In Denmark, for example, section 16, paragraph 3 of the Agriculture Act[28] provides that the maximum number of agricultural holdings which may be owned by the owner, his spouse and children under 18 is three. This provision prevents persons (in practice women) whose spouse already owes 3 agricultural holdings

---

[26] COM(2003)657 and SEC(2003)1213 which contains an Extended Impact Assessment of the proposal.

[27] 86/613/EEC on the application of the principle of equal treatment between men and women engaged in an activity, including agriculture, in a self-employed capacity, and on the protection of self-employed women during pregnancy and motherhood. The Directive should have been implemented by 30.6.1989.

[28] Consolidated Act no 598 of 15.7.1999.

from aquiring a Danish farm.[29] In my view, this provision is unlawful under the above 1986 directive. In 2003 a proposal was put forward to abolish this discrimination as part of a more general reform simplifying Danish agricultural legislation.[30]

4.2.2. Access to Venture Capital and Credit Facilities

Research from the US suggests that there is a funding gap in women-led ventures. In a report on the Diana project[31] it is stated that in 2000, estimates were that women owned *38 percent* of all businesses in the US, or roughly 9 million businesses. The reported numbers suggest that between 1953 and 1998, venture capital financing went to approximately 7,916 male-led businesses and 395 female-led businesses (*4.8 percent* of the total). Further breakdown of these numbers reveals that in 1997, the proportion of deals going to women-led firms was *2.5 percent* with an increase to *5 percent* in 2001.

An analysis of the Danish Agency for Trade and Industry from 2000 revealed the folllowing barriers for women entrepreneurs' access to bank loans in the starting phase of a business:[32] One important criterion for banks is confidence, and this is established among other things by the bank's previous knowledge of the entrepreneur before he or she approaches the bank to apply for a loan for starting his or her own enterprise. The fact that the banks often do not know the (potential) woman entrepreneur personally, or even may not have seen her before the day she comes to the bank, is seen as an important barrier both for the woman entrepreneur and for the bank.

Men are often better at establishing and maintaining professional relations, and there are countless male networks, formal as well as informal. In such a network the men's position and the preparation for starting an enterprise are strengthened considerably. There are also several, good female networks, but since so few women are leaders or starters of enterprises, the networks are less conspicuous. Generally, women do not base their working life as much on

---

[29] See on women's access to agricultural holdings in Denmark Neergaard, Ulla: Landbrugsloven på kant med EU retten?, U 2002 B 213.

[30] L 113: Forslag til lov om landbrugsejendomme. See also Betænkning nr 1429, July 2003. Forenklinger i jordlovgivningen.

[31] The Diana Project. Women business owners and equity capital: the myths dispelled, at http://www.entreworld.org/Bookstore/PDFs/RE-032.pdf. See generally on the Diana project www.esbri.se/diana.asp.

[32] The Relations of Banks to Women Entrepreneurs. The Analysis of The Danish Agency for Trade and Industry: Women Entrepreneurs now and in the Future, Published by the Danish Agency for Trade and Industry September 2000, available online at http://www.efs.dk/publikationer/ rappor ter/bankers.uk/index -e ng .h tm l.

networks as much as men do, and as a consequence women may have less back up and support in the establishing phase.

Another barrier that caught the consultants' attention was the fact that women entrepreneurs often apply for financing of small projects. These women entrepreneurs are often referred to private customer departments or bank advisers who deal with quite small business cases exclusively. This type of bank adviser does not always possess the necessary experience in considering the application on any other basis than some policy-related guidelines, and this may easily lead the bank adviser to take a too narrow view of the project for which money is sought, and this again may lead to a refusal of the loan.

A further identified barrier was that a young, male business consultant in the bank may find it difficult to understand the projects of women entrepreneurs who are often 10 to 20 years older. A better age match will improve communication and understanding, whereas the participants do not find it important that consultant and applicant are of the same sex, but for the women who prefer female consultants it should be made clear that they have the option.

Since the women have rarely become "a familiar face" in the corporate department, a good dialogue requires the bank adviser to take time to get acquainted with the woman. According to the consultants, the banks are rarely prepared for this. At the same time it is often an unaccustomed situation for the woman to visit the bank, a fact that does not make the dialogue easier at the first loan meeting.

5. Scope of the ban on discrimination in contracts for the provision of goods and services

5.1. Who are entitled not to be discriminated against? All Persons

Article1(2) of the proposed Directive[33] on equal treatment in the access to and supply of goods and services provides that the Directive shall apply to *all persons* in relation to the access to and the supply of goods and services which are available to the public, including housing, as regards both the public and private sectors, including public bodies. The term 'all persons' is not defined in the proposed Directive. In the following I will discuss its coverage in relation to persons making use of the free movement of goods and services provision in the EU, EU citizens, third country nationals residing lawfully in the EU and others.

It must be assumed that a violation of the Directive must have some connection with the EU in order for the alleged victim to be able to make claims

---

[33] COM(2003)657.

for compensation or other remedies with reference to the directive, see on enforcement below in Chapter 5.

5.1.1. Persons making use of the free movement provisions
In order for a person to be able to invoke the EU free movement provisions the case must have some cross-border aspect. If the proposed Directive had only aimed at securing the functioning of the internal market its personal scope of application could have been limited to the limited group of persons engaged in free movement.

5.1.2. EU citizens
The proposed Directive is, however, as mentioned, mainly aimed at safeguarding fundamental rights. In the Preamble[34] to the proposed Directive it is stated that the right to equality before the law and protection against discrimination for all persons constitutes a universal right recognised by the Universal Declaration of Human Rights, the United Nations Convention on the Elimination of all forms of Discrimination Against Women, the International Convention on the Elimination of all forms of Racial Discrimination and the United Nations Covenants on Civil and Political Rights and on Economic, Social and Cultural Rights and by the European Convention for the Protection of Human Rights and Fundamental Freedoms, to which all Member States are signatories.

Against this background, it would appear that the scope of the proposed directive covers more persons than those entitled to free movement under the EU provisions on free movement of goods and services. The term 'all persons' in the context of a the proposed directive must at least cover all EU citizens who generally enjoy the fundamental rights guaranteed by the Community.

5.1.3. Other persons
It probably also goes further than the concept of Union citizenship and includes at least those third country nationals who are lawfully residing in the territory of the EU. It probably also includes other third country nationals, including illegal immigrants and others with no legal right to be in the EU in relation to contracts where the lack of lawful residence in the EU is not relevant. If for example an illegal, male immigrant is required to pay (in cash) a higher price to enter a discotheque than a woman he is probably entitled to claim reparation or compensation under the proposed Directive.

---

[34] See recital 2.

5.1.4. Both recipients and providers of goods and services

The proposed Directive covers as mentioned both consumer and commercial contracts and therefore protects both providers, typically sellers, of goods and services and recipients, typically buyers, of goods and services.

5.2. Who has a Duty to Comply with the Principle of Gender Equality

As other directives, the proposed directive will not be directly binding[35] for private service providers, etc but there will be a duty on the part of the Member States to ensure that relevant persons comply with the obligations required by the directive. It is not specified in the directive exactly who those relevant persons are. To some extent an answer to that question can be deduced from the material scope of the directive, see just below.

5.3. Substantive scope: Contracts for the Provision of Goods and Services

5.3.1. Background

The Commission has held discussions on the the proposed Directive on equal treatment between women and men in the access to and supply of goods and services with various stakeholders on issues which might be covered in such a Directive. In earlier drafts for a proposal it was intended to cover a fairly broad scope, more or less similar to the Directive on ethnic and racial equality[36] which prohibits ethnic and racial discrimination both in access to and supply of goods and services and in a number of other areas including the labour market. Lobbying conducted by vested interests, in particular the insurance and the media industry, delayed the adoption of a formal proposal on gender equality outside the labour market and resulted in a narrowing of its material scope.[37] Education, taxation[38] and the content of the media were left out.

---

[35] See on direct effect above in Chapter 2.

[36] 2000/43/EC.

[37] See for example European Women's News Lobby Flash June 2003, http://www.womenlobby.org/.

[38] As regards taxation, the Commission now holds the view that, as a result of the direct effect and material scope of Article 141 EC, existing Community law requires the taxation of income from employment to respect the principle of equal treatment. Member States are therefore already obliged to ensure that their tax system does not discriminate against members of one sex or the other. It is therefore, in the view of the Commission, not necessary for the Community to intervene further to regulate the taxation of employment income, see further COM(2003)657 p 5.

To avoid conflict with other fundamental freedoms such as the freedom and plurality of the media, Article 1 provides that it does not apply to the content of media and advertising. Nor does the Directive apply to education, which is to a large extent already covered by existing Community law.

In respect of the media sector and education the Commission still thinks further legislation may be necessary but it needs more time and further negotiations with stakeholders to achieve sufficient consensus on these issues.

5.3.2. Goods and services

As a result of the above consideration, the proposal for a Directive implementing the principle of equal treatment between women and men presented in November 2003 is limited to the access to and supply of goods and services.

Services is used in the usual Community law meaning of the concept. In the explanatory remarks to the proposed Directive on equal treatment between men and women[39] it is stated that the concept of goods and services has the same meaning as in the Race discrimination directive[40] and should be restricted to those which are normally provided for remuneration.

It covers access to premises into which the public are permitted to enter.

It also encompasses all types of (commercial) housing, including rented accommodation and accommodation in hotels. In the Staff Working Paper on the proposed directive on equal treatment in the access to and supply of goods and services sexual harassment by landlords is mentioned as an example of unlawful discrimination in violation of the proposed Directive.[41] The proposed Directive does not apply to transactions which are carried out in a purely private context, such as, for example, the renting of a holiday home to a family member or the letting of a room in a private house.

Services such as banking, insurance and other financial services are core areas of the proposed ban on sex discrimination. Most of the examples of discrimination mentioned in the preparatory works are from the financial sector.

Transport and the the services of any profession or trade will also be covered of the material scope of teh proposed directive.

6. Public Procurement

The substantive rules in the EC Treaty on free movement are, in matters of public procurement, complemented with 4 Directives coordinating tendering

---

[39] COM(2003)756 p 13.

[40] 2000/43/EC.

[41] SEC(2003)1213 p 5.

procedures in respect of supplies, works, services and utilities[42] and two remedies Directives.[43] In February 2004, a new directive amending the substantive procurement directives was adopted.[44] It is stated in Recital 1 of the preamble that this Directive is based on ECJ case-law, in particular case-law on award criteria, which clarifies the possibilities for the contracting authorities to meet the needs of the public concerned, including in the environmental and/or social area, provided that such criteria are linked to the subject-matter of the contract, do not confer an unrestricted freedom of choice on the contracting authority, are expressly mentioned and comply with the fundamental principles mentioned in Recital 2, in particular the principle of freedom of movement of goods, the principle of freedom of establishment and the principle of freedom to provide services and to the principles deriving therefrom, such as the principle of equal treatment, the principle of non-discrimination, the principle of mutual recognition, the principle of proportionality and the principle of transparency, ie the fundamental economic rights rather than the fundamental human rights. Gender equality is not specifically mentioned

Within the limits set by the ban on discrimination on grounds of nationality contracting authorities can choose what sort of work and contract they will put out to tender. This means that they have discretion to choose a contract containing staff requirements (number, qualification, etc) and conditions that promote employment policies including labour clauses. All conditions must be made public from the outset and cannot be negotiated with individual contractors. The procedural requirements of the Procurement Directives must be

---

[42] 93/36/EEC, OJ 1993 L 199/1, coordinating procedures for the award of public supply contracts, 93/37/EEC, concerning the coordination of procedures for the award of public works contracts, 92/50/EEC, OJ 1992 L 209/1, relating to the coordination of procedures for the award of public(services), 93/38/EEC, OJ 1993 L 199/94, coordinating the procurement procedures of entities operating in the water, energy, transport and telecommunications sectors. Those directives were in 1997 amended by directive 97/52/EC.

[43] 89/665/EEC, OJ 1989 L 395/33, on the coordination of the laws, regulations and administrative provisions relating to the application of review procedures for the award of public supply and public works contracts and 92/13/EEC, OJ 1992 L 76/14, coordinating the laws, regulations and administrative provisions relating to the application of Community rules on the procurement procedures of entities operating in the water, energy, transport and telecommunications sectors.

[44] At the time of writing the new directive is awaiting publication in the Official Journal. The Joint text approved by the Conciliation Committee provided for in Article 251(4) EC is available at http://www2.europarl.eu.int/omk/sipade2? PUBREF=-//EP/ /NONSGML+DOC-C+C5-2003-0607+0+DOC+PDF+V0//EN&L=EN&LEVEL= 2&NAV=S&LSTDOC=Y.

observed. This means that potential contractors must first be assessed as to their suitability to perform the contract. Among the tenderers who are capable of performing the contract it must be awarded either on the basis of the lowest price only or the 'economically most advantageous' offer. If the contracting authority has chosen lowest price only as award criterion employment related criteria cannot be taken into consideration whereas this - arguably - is lawful when the award criterion is the 'economically most advantageous' offer.

In 2001, the Commission issued an interpretive communication on the Community law applicable to public procurement and the possibilities for integrating social considerations into public procurement.[45] The expression 'social considerations' used in this Communication covers a very wide range of issues and fields. It can mean measures to ensure compliance with fundamental rights, with the principle of equality of treatment and non-discrimination for example, between men and women.

6.1. Exclusion of candidates or tenderers for non-compliance with gender equality legislation

The Commission takes the view in the above Communication that the public procurement directives currently in force contain provisions that permit the exclusion, at the selection stage, of candidates or tenderers who breach national social legislation, including those relevant to the promotion of equality of opportunities.

6.2. Execution of the contract

Contracting authorities can impose contractual clauses relating to the manner in which a contract will be executed. The execution phase of public procurement contracts is not currently regulated by the public procurement directives. However, the clauses or conditions regarding execution of the contract must comply with Community law and, in particular, not discriminate directly or indirectly against non-national tenderers. Such clause can include the obligation to implement, during the execution of the contract, measures that are designed to promote equality between men and women.

---

[45] COM(2001)566.

7. Marketing and Advertising

7.1. Sex discriminatory advertisements

The ban on sex discrimination in national equality legislation described above in Chapter 2 usually covers sex discriminatory advertisements. The Norwegian Marketing Practices Act section 1(2) contains a particularly detailed provision:[46]

> The advertiser and anyone who makes advertising material shall ensure that the advertisement is not inconsistent with the principle of the equality of men and women and that it does not exploit the body of one of the sexes or express an offensive or degrading assessment of either sex.

There is a ban on sex discrimination in advertisements in Article 12(b) in the Television Directive[47] but sex discriminatory advertisements in other media than television are not prohibited at Community level and, as set out above, the proposed Directive on equal treatment in the provision of goods and services will not cover the content of advertising.

Many statements in advertisements are contractually relevant. They may for example constitute binding offers (as opposed to invitations to make offers) or be decisive for whether there is a defect[48] or a guarantee.[49]

---

[46] My translation from Norwegian. The Norwegian Marketing Practices Act is available (in Norwegian) at http://www.lovdata.no/all/tl-19720616-047-001.html. Section 1(1) and (2) of the Norwegian Marketing Practices Act reads:
'I næringsvirksomhet må det ikke foretas handling som strider mot god forretnings-skikk næringsdrivende imellom, eller er urimelig i forhold til forbrukere eller som for øvrig strider mot god markedsføringsskikk.
Annonsør og den som utformer reklame skal sørge for at reklame ikke er i strid med likeverdet mellom kjønnene, og at den ikke utnytter det ene kjønns kropp eller gir inntrykk av en støtende eller nedsettende vurdering av kvinne eller mann.'
See generally on this provision Graver, Kjersti: Norwegian regulation on sex. discriminatory advertising, in Krämer, Ludwig, Hans Micklitz and Hans Tonner(eds) Law and Diffuse Interests in the European Legal Order, Liber amicorum Norbert Reich, Baden-Baden 1997 p 429.

[47] Council Directive 89/552/EEC of 3 October 1989 on the coordination of certain provisions laid down by Law, Regulation or Administrative Action in Member States concerning the pursuit of television broadcasting activities.

[48] Article 2(2)(d) of the Consumer Sales Directive 1999/44/EC provides that consumer goods are presumed to be in conformity with the contract if they show the quality and performance which are normal in goods of the same type and which the consumer can reasonably expect, given the nature of the goods and taking into account any public

The purpose of the exclusion of advertisements from the scope of the proposed Directive on equal treatment in the provision of goods and services was to ensure that the concern for the fundamental right to gender equality does not encroach upon the - in some instances conflicting - fundamental right to freedom of expression in the media, for example the freedom to portray men and women in a sexy way in advertisements.

The scope of the exclusion for advertisements must be interpreted in the light of this background. The purpose was only to allow a portrayal of men and women in a way that some consider to be harassment or sexual harassment.

The right to freedom of expression cannot legitimize that other kinds of sex discrimination, for example price differentiation by sex or differences in guarantees provided to men and women, should become lawful just because they are placed in an advertisement.

7.2. Gender-based promotional offers

Sex-based differences in promotional offers is unlawful under existing national bans on sex discrimination will be covered by the proposed Directive. In the Irish *Icon Night Club* case the policy of giving free entrance on Thursday night to women was adopted for promotional reasons. That didn't make it lawful.[50]

8. Validity

8.1. Duress

The Italian Civil Code contains provisions on duress (Violenza in Italian) in art 1434 and 1435. Article 1434 of the Civil Code provides that duress is cause for annulment of a contract even if exerted by a third person. Under Article 1435 of the Civil Code on the Characteristics of duress:

---

statements on the specific characteristics of the goods made about them by the seller, the producer or his representative, particularly in advertising or on labelling.

[49] Article 1(2)(e) of the Consumer Sales Directive 1999/44/EC defines a guaranteee in the following way: (e) guarantee: shall mean any undertaking by a seller or producer to the consumer, given without extra charge, to reimburse the price paid or to replace, repair or handle consumer goods in any way if they do not meet the specifications set out in the guarantee statement or in the relevant advertising.

[50] The Irish decision is available at www.odei.ie/2004%20Equal%20Status/DEC-S2004-001.pdf. A similar case is pending before the Danish Complaints Board for Equality.

Duress must be of such a nature as to impress a reasonable person and to cause him to fear that he or his property will be exposed to an unjust and considerable injury. In this respect, the age, *sex* and condition of the persons shall be considered[51]

In the other EU countries sex is not explicitly mentioned in the corresponding provisions on duress but the rule is probably the same.

8.2. Undue influence

Gender aspect of undue influence has been particularly discussed with regard to consumer surety contracts.

The Commission proposed a Directive on credit for consumers in 2002[52] which for the first time will harmonise consumer surety contract law in Europe. The proposed directive provides for protection of personal guarantors by giving them the same right to same information as the borrower.

The proposal leaves the gender aspect totally unmentioned even though - as set out in chapter 2 the Commission has a gender mainstreaming duty - and the law on surety contracts would appear to be an area where a gender mainstreaming exercise would be fairly easy because the gender aspect has already been discussed in academic literature and case law at the highest national level.

The legal situation of surety wives, particularly in the UK, has already been discussed in academic writing[53] and in case law.

For many years, the British courts have been confronted with cases where they had to balance the need, on the one hand, of lenders (usually banks) to be able to lend money on the security of family homes and, on the other, the need

---

[51] The English translation is taken from Gordley, James(Editor). Enforceability of Promises in European Contract Law. Port Chester, NY, USA: Cambridge University Press, 2001, p 228. The Italian original reads: Art 1434 Violenza. La violenza è causa di annullamento del contratto, anche se esercitata da un terzo. Art 1435 Caratteri della violenza. La violenza deve essere di tal natura da far impressione sopra una persona sensata è da farle temere di esporre se o i suoi beni a un male ingiusto è notevole. Si ha riguardo, in questa materia, all'età, al sesso e alla condizione delle persone.

[52] COM(2002)443. Proposal for a Directive of the European Parliament and of the Council on the harmonisation of the laws, regulations and administrative provisions of the Member States concerning credit for consumers.

[53] See for example Debra Morris: Surety Wives in the House of Lords: Time for Solicitors to `Get Real'? *Royal Bank of Scotland plc* v. *Etridge (No. 2)* [2001] 4 All E.R. 449, Feminist Legal Studies 2003 p 57, Geary, David: Notes on Family Guarantees in English and Scottish Law - A Comment, European Review of Private Law 2000 p 25 and Fehlberg, Belinda: Sexually transmitted debt - Surety experience and English law, Oxford 1997.

to protect the vulnerable (usually wives) who may have unwittingly put their homes at risk. This issue has now been decided by the House of Lords in 2001 in a number of conjoined appeals concerning the validity of a bank's charge over the matrimonial home. In most out of the cases, a wife charged her interest in the home as security for her husband's business debts. The loan was not repaid and the lender sought possession. Each wife then alleged that her signature on the lender's charge had been obtained by the undue influence of her husband, that the bank was on notice of this, and that the charge should therefore be set aside.

In Royal Bank of Scotland v Etridge (AP)[54] the House of Lords set out procedures to be followed by lenders in order to counter any argument by the wife that the contract should be set aside because her signature has been obtained by the undue influence of her husband. The House of Lords held that whenever the relationship between the debtor and surety is a 'non-commercial' one, such as when a wife offers to stand surety for her husband's debts the wife should receive independent advice.

The information and advice duties for lenders prescribed in Article 6 of the proposed directive on credit for consumers do not - as required by the House of Lords in respect of English law on surety wives - include a requirement of independent advice. The proposal will therefore lower the standard of protection for surety wives compared with the standard established in English case law[55] without any discussion of why this group should receive less favourable treatment than it used to.

The proposal for a new consumer credit directive has so far not progressed much through the legislative process. The Economic and Social Committee has recommended that the Council and the Member States do not accept the proposal for a directive as it currently stands.[56] The Committee does not specifically mention the gender aspect but it critizises that the proposal does not fully uphold existing standards of consumer protection.

8.3. Good faith and fair dealing

In a comparative perspective one of the distinctive features of civil law jurisdictions is that they provide for a general requirement of good faith - see

---

[54] http://www.parliament.the-stationery-office.co.uk/pa/ld200102/ldjudgmt/jd011011/et ridg-1.htm, 11 October 2001 [2001] UKHL 44

[55] The proposed directive is based on the method of total harmonisation. It will therefore not be possible for a Member State to uphold a higher standard of protection for sureties.

[56] OH 2003 C 234.

eg BGB § 242[57] and the French Code Civil art 1134[58] - whereas no such general requirement of good faith exists in the English common law.[59] In the Nordic countries Section 36 of the Nordic Contracts Act provides for a test of reasonableness. An agreement may be amended or set aside, in whole or in part, if its enforcement would be unreasonable or contrary to principles of fair conduct. The same applies to other legal transactions.

The above general clauses have so far not - explicitly - been interpreted as comprising the principle of gender equality. As mentioned above in Chapter 2 it is a widely shared assumption that freedom of contract and (mandatory) gender equality are irreconcilable. A leading commentary on the BGB thus states:[60]

'While civil law is governed by the principle of personal autonomy, it is impossible to derive a general obligation of equal treatment either from Article 3 GG (constitution) nor from para. 242 BGB (Civil Code)[1]'

When making a decision under section 36 of the Nordic Contracts Acts, the courts are to consider not only (1) conditions at the time of contracting but also (2) subsequent developments and (3) the content of the contract. There is thus a dynamic perspective in section 36. In this respect the Directive on unfair terms in consumer contracts[62] is more static in that it only requires voidability of terms which were unfair already at the time of the conclusion of the contract.

---

[57] Which provides: 'Der Schuldner ist verpflichtet, die Leistung so zu bewirken, wie Treu und Glauben mit Rücksicht auf die Verkehrssitte es erfordern.'

[58] Which provides: 'Les conventions légalement formées tiennent lieu de loi à ceux qui les ont faites. Elles ne peuvent être révoquées que de leur consentement mutuel, ou pour les causes que la loi autorise. Elles doivent être exécutées de bonne foi'.

[59] Cf Hesselink, M: 'Good Faith' in AS Hartkamp, M W Hesselink, E H Hondius, C Joustra and E du Perron (eds): Towards a European Civil Code, Kluwer Law International 1998 p 285

[60] Palandt, Otto et al (eds), Bürgerliches Gesetzbuch, 2001, quoted from the translation in Schiek, Dagmar: Torn between Arithmetic and Substantive Equality? Perspectives on Equality in German Labour Law, The International Journal of Comparative Labour Law and Industrial Relations 2002 p 149. See for a critical viw on this position Schiek, Dagmar: Differenzierte Gerechtigkeit. Diskriminierungsschutz und Vertragsrecht, Baden-Baden 2000.

[61] BGB § 242 provides: 'Der Schuldner ist verpflichtet, die Leistung so zu bewirken, wie Treu und Glauben mit Rücksicht auf die Verkehrssitte es erfordern.'.

[62] 93/13/EEC.

Article 3 of the directive stipulates that a contractual term which has not been individually negotiated shall be regarded as unfair if, contrary to the requirement of good faith, it causes a significant imbalance in the parties' rights and obligations arising under the contract, to the detriment of the consumer. A term shall always be regarded as not individually negotiated where it has been drafted in advance and the consumer has therefore not been able to influence the substance of the term, particularly in the context of a pre-formulated standard contract. The Annex to the Directive contains an indicative and non-exhaustive list of the terms which may be regarded as unfair. This list does not mention discrimination.[63]

As set out above in Chapter 2, it follows from the general principles of Community law that there is a duty upon the national courts to respect the principle of gender equality when they are acting within the sphere of EU law. To the extent the above general clauses in national contract law are used to implement EU directives, such as for example the directive on unfair terms in consumer contracts, there is therefore a duty under Community law to read the principle of gender equality into the general clauses. As explained above in Chapter 3, the national courts are also, in the exercise of their capacity as Community courts, bound directly by the gender mainstreaming obligation in Article 3(2) EC.

8.4. The proposed Directive on equal treatment in the provision of goods and services

Some violations of the ban on sex discrimination in the provision of goods and services consist in contracts being concluded on discriminatory terms. Those terms will be null and void and will have to be amended once the proposed Directive has been adopted. Article 12 (b) of the proposed Directive on equal treatment in the provision of goods and services provides that any provisions contrary to the principle of equal treatment included in individual or collective contracts or agreements, internal rules of undertakings, and rules governing profit making or non-profit-making associations are, or may be declared, null and void or are amended.

This article is a classic provision, contained in all previous Community instruments on discrimination, which concerns compliance with the Directive by the Member States. Equal treatment involves the elimination of discrimination arising from any laws, regulations or administrative provision and the

---

[63] The indicative list has not been transposed into a statutory text in Danish or Swedish law but is only mentioned in the preparatory works. The EU Commission initiated infringement proceedings against Sweden on that ground but in 2002, the ECJ dismissed the action, see Case C-478/99, *Commission* v *Sweden* [2002] ECR I-4147.

Directive therefore requires the Member States to abolish any such provisions. As with earlier legislation, the Directive also requires that any provisions contrary to the principle of equal treatment must be rendered null and void or amended, or must be capable of being so rendered if they are challenged.

In *Kowalska*,[64] the AG discussed the effects of any finding of incompatibility on the freedom of contract enjoyed by the parties to a collective agreement. The question was whether, in the event that a contested article of the collective agreement was declared incompatible with Community law, part-time workers become entitled to a severance grant proportionate to the hours they work or, conversely, whether the freedom of contract of the parties to a collective agreement precludes conferment of such a right.

In *Defrenne*(2)[65] and in *Commission* v *UK*[66] concerning the Equal Treatment Directive the ECJ held that the directive covers all collective agreements without distinction as to the nature of the legal effects which they do or do not produce. The reason for that generality lies in the fact that, even if they are not legally binding as between the parties who sign them or with regard to the employment relationships which they govern, collective agreements nevertheless have important de facto consequences for the employment relationships to which they refer, particularly in so far as they determine the rights of the workers and, in the interests of industrial harmony, give undertakings some indication of the conditions which employment relationships must satisfy or need not satisfy. The need to ensure that the directive is completely effective therefore requires that any clauses in such agreements which are incompatible with the obligations imposed by the directive upon the member states may be rendered inoperative, eliminated or amended by appropriate means.

9. Gender Related Terms in Contracts, Business Conditions etc

9.1. Duty to take both sexes into account

In *Rummler v Dato Druck GmbH*,[67] the applicant challenged the classifications used in the framework wage-rate agreement for the German printing industry. She argued that her work should have been placed in a different category since she was obliged to lift heavy weights which for women represented heavy

---

[64] Case C-33/89, *Kowalska* [1990] ECR I-2591.

[65] Case 43/75, *Sabena* (No 2) [1976] ECR 455.

[66] Case 165/82, *Commission* v *United Kingdom* [1983] ECR 3431.

[67] Case 237/ 85, *Rummler* [1986] ECR 2101.

physical work. The ECJ ruled that Article 1 of the Equal Pay Directive does not preclude the use of factors such as physical effort which may favour one sex provided that overall the job evaluation scheme does not discriminate on grounds of sex. In order for a job evaluation scheme not to be discriminatory as a whole it must, in so far as the tasks carried out in the undertaking permit, take into account criteria for which workers of each sex may show particular aptitude. If, for example, both physical strength and dexterity are relevant for a job, both criteria must be taken into account in a a job evaluation scheme.

Applied on areas outside of employment the principle in *Rummler* implies, for example, that a credit-rating system must include relevant criteria to the advantage of both sexes.

9.2. Price discrimination

As a starting point it is clearly unlawful - when sex discrimination is prohibited - to charge different prices for men and women for the same goods or services. In the Irish *Icon Night Club* case[68] where there were different price conditions for men and women the Equality Officer thus found, that the practice of charging males an entrance fee on a Thursday night and allowing females in free was discriminatory, in that the respondent treated the complainant less favourably than females in similar circumstances. She concluded that the complainant did establish a prima facie case of discriminatory treatment. She also concluded that the action of the respondent was not a positive measure allowed under Section 14 of the Act, but the action was a measure taken for commercial reasons aimed at attracting more customers to the business. She awarded the complainant €10 and free entry to the night club for 7 nights. She also ordered the respondent to review his entrance policies to comply with the requirements of the Equal Status Act, 2000.

9.3. Actuarial factors

In the Commission Staff Working Paper underlying the proposal[69] for a Directive on equal treatment in the provision of goods and services it is concluded that differences of treatment of women and men is widespread in the insurance sector which either disadvantage members of one sex in terms of

---

[68] Decision DEC-S2004-001, available at www.odei.ie/2004%20 Equal%20Status/ DEC-S2004-001.pdf. A similar case is pending before the Danish Complaints Board for Equality, see www.ligenaevn.dk.

[69] See SEC(2003)1213 p 8, 10, 18 and 19.

access to the insurance cover provided or which lead to disadvantage in the level of benefits paid out.

Insurance based on gender related actuarial factors is particularly often used in motor car insurance, health insurance and life annuities.

Such discrimination is explicitly exempted in the UK SDA, see above in Chapter 2. In the other countries it is less clear whether and to what extent sex discrimination by reference to actuarial factors is lawful under current legislation but in practice such discrimination occurs.

9.3.1. The proposed Directive on equal treatment in the provision of goods and services

Article 4 of the the proposed Directive on equal treatment in the access to and supply of goods and services specifically targets sex discrimination based on actuarial factors. It provides:

> 1. Member States shall ensure that the use of sex as a factor in the calculation of premiums and benefits for the purpose of insurance and related financial services is prohibited in all new contracts concluded after [date referred to in Article 16(1)] at the latest.
> 2. Member States may defer implementation of the measures necessary to comply with paragraph 1 until [six years after date referred to in paragraph 1] at the latest. In that case, the Member States concerned shall immediately inform the Commission. They shall compile, publish and regularly update comprehensive tables on the mortality and life expectancy of women and men.

9.3.2. Direct discrimination - justification on economic grounds?

One of the obvious group differences between men and women is that women in EU Member States on average live longer than men. In a number of EU countries occupational pension schemes must use unisex calculations.[70] The Commission's work programme for 2003 includes an initiative to recast the existing gender equality directives in employment and occupation.[71] In the on-going discussion on recasting the gender equality directives one of the issues is whether to make unisex pension services mandatory in employment and occupation.

Private pension contracts, where the employer is not a party to the agreement, for example a pension agreement a worker or a self-employed makes with a bank or an insurance company may (probably) under the law of most EU Member

---

[70] See for details the Commission's pension report from 2003 at http://europa.eu.int/comm/employment_social/.

[71] See COM(2003) 98, Annual Report on Equal Opportunities for Women and Men in the European Union 2002.

States be calculated on the basis of actuarial factors so that a woman and a man with the same individual characteristics, solely on ground of their belonging to different gender groups, cannot obtain the same contract.[72]

As set out above in Chapter 3 direct sex discrimination occurs when *one person* is treated less favourably on grounds of sex than another is, has been or would be treated in a comparable situation.

If the prohibition against direct discrimination is interpreted as requiring individual treatment as opposed to group treatment and if - in accordance with the orthodox position in EU law - no justification on economic grounds is accepted with regard to direct discrimination, the use of gender-related actuarial factors in calculating the terms of insurance and pension contracts is unlawful in legal systems where sex discrimination in the provision of financial services is prohibited.

It is, however, as set out in Chapter 3, contested that there is no defence against direct discrimination. As the proposed Directive is worded it will not be possible to justify the use of gender-related actuarial factors.

10. Data Processing

In the following I discuss to what extent the law makes it unlawful for a business to process data related to gender in connection with contracting in a way that either intrudes upon an individual's privacy or facilitates direct or indirect sex discrimination or harassment or sexual harassment.

10.1. The legal framework

10.1.1. The draft Constitution
Article 8 of the EU Charter on Fundamental Rights provides:

> Protection of personal data
> 1. Everyone has the right to the protection of personal data concerning him or her.
> 2. Such data must be processed fairly for specified purposes and on the basis of the consent of the person concerned or some other legitimate basis laid down by law. Everyone has the right of access
> to data which has been collected concerning him or her, and the right to have it rectified.
> 3. Compliance with these rules shall be subject to control by an independent authority.

The draft EU Constitution includes, as set out in Chapter 2, the EU Charter on Fundamental Rights as an integral part of the Constitution for the EU. In addition Article I-50 of the draft Constitution provides:

---

[72] Luckhaus, Linda: Privatisation and Pensions: Some Pitfalls for Women? European Law Journal 1997 p 83.

Protection of personal data
1. Everyone has the right to the protection of personal data concerning him or her.
2. A European law shall lay down the rules relating to the protection of individuals with regard to the processing of personal data by Union Institutions, bodies and agencies, and by the Member States when carrying out activities which come under the scope of Union law, and the rules relating to the free movement of such data. Compliance with these rules shall be subject to the control of an independent authority.

10.1.2. The Data Protection Directive

In 1995, the Directive[73] on the protection of individuals with regard to the processing of personal data and on the free movement of such data was adopted. It is a combination of a human rights directive and a free movement directive. It protects, at the same time, the privacy as enshrined in Article 8 ECHR of physical persons and the free movement of data related to physical persons.

It is a general directive applying to nearly all areas of life, including contracting but not specifically adapted to situations concerning contractual relations. There is not yet any case law clarifying the consequences of the Directive in matters of contract or gender equality.

10.2. Purpose of the data protection rules

In official documents and academic literature[74] on data protection there is a narrow focus on privacy protection and practically no discussion of how much or little protection there is of other fundamental rights (eg the right not to be discriminated against on grounds of sex or the freedom of expression) in connection with processing of personal data. The right to privacy is one (important) example of a fundamental right protected by the directive. It is specifically mentioned in the Directive and is also guaranteed in Article 8 ECHR and Article 7 of the EU Charter on Fundamental Rights.[75]

The wording of the Data Protection Directive shows clearly that informational privacy is not the one and only fundamental right protected by the Directive. Recital 2 of the preamble stes that data-processing systems are designed to serve man. They must, whatever the nationality or residence of natural persons, respect their fundamental rights and freedoms, notably the right to privacy, and contribute to economic and social progress, trade expansion and the well-being

---

[73] 95/46/EC.

[74] See for example Blume, Peter: Protection of informational privacy, Copenhagen 2002.

[75] Article 7 reads: Respect for private and family life. Everyone has the right to respect for his or her private and family life, home and communications.

of individuals. Articel 1(1) of the Data Protection Directive provides that Member States (emphasis added):

> Object of the Directive
> 1. In accordance with this Directive, Member States shall protect the *fundamental rights* and freedoms of natural persons, and in particular their right to privacy with respect to the processing of personal data.
> 2. Member States shall neither restrict nor prohibit the free flow of personal data between Member States for reasons connected with the protection afforded under paragraph 1.

The provision in Article 7(f) of the Directive on, the so-called balance of interest test, also describes the protected interests of the data subject as his or her fundamental rights in plural not just as the data subject's interest in privacy protection. The fundamental rights and freedoms protected by the directive must therefore include all kinds of fundamental rights which may be infringed by processing of personal data including the fundamental right not to be discriminated against on grounds of sex (directly or indirectly, harassed or sexually harassed).

10.3. Definitions

10.3.1. Personal data
Article 2 of the Directive defines its key concepts. For the purposes of the Directive 'personal data' means any information relating to an identified or identifiable natural person ('data subject').

Information that an identifiable natural person is male or female or belongs to a particular gender group (pregnant women, single mothers, etc) is personal data within the meaning of the directive.

10.3.2. Gender profiling
Profiling is not defined in the data protection directive. Profiling is the inference of a set of characteristics (profile) about an individual person or collective entity and the subsequent treatment of that person/entity or other persons/entities in the light of these characteristics.[76]

Profiling can target an individual (man or woman), an organised collective entity (eg a woman-owned firm) or a non-organised entity (eg all men or all

---

[76] See further Bygrave, Lee: Data protection law - approaching its rationale, logic and limits, Dordrecht, 2002 p 301 *et seq.*

women or a gender group). Bygrave[77] distinguishes between abstract profiling and specific profiling. Abstract profiling involves the inference of a set of characteristics about a relatively abstract category of persons (eg, male university students or large multinational corporations). Specific profiling involves the inference of a set of characteristics about a specific individual or organised collective entity on the basis of data related to that person/entity.

The data on the basis of which profiles are generated can come from a variety of sources: they can be collected from the data subject, eg pursuant to a sales transaction or from databases maintained by the profiler or third parties. The latter type of data can be generally available or relatively confidential, eg customer lists. For the purpose of abstract profiling none of the data need to be capable of revealing the identity of a specific individual. Specific profiling will require at least some data capable of revealing the identity of a specific individual or collective entity.

Both abstract and specific profiling can be used for many purposes. The most common in a business context is targeted marketing of goods and services, see above on market segmentation by gender. Another common purpose is credit assessment. Profiling can enhance identification of persons who are likely to default on their loan repayments.

The techniques (data warehousing, data-mining, artificial neural networks, intelligent agents, etc) used for profiling are becoming more sophisticated with the growth in electronic commerce.

10.3.3. Processing of personal data
Processing of personal data is a broad concept. It means any operation or set of operations which is performed upon personal data, whether or not by automatic means, such as collection, recording, organization, storage, adaptation or alteration, retrieval, consultation, use, disclosure by transmission, dissemination or otherwise making available, alignment or combination, blocking, erasure or destruction.

10.3.4. Consent
The data subject's consent means any freely given specific and informed indication of his wishes by which the data subject signifies his agreement to personal data relating to him being processed. An employee's consent must thus be freely given specific and informed in order to justify data processing.

---

[77] Op cit p 303.

10.4. Scope

Article 3 on the scope of the data protection directive provides that it shall apply to the processing of personal data wholly or partly by automatic means, and to the processing otherwise than by automatic means of personal data which form part of a filing system or are intended to form part of a filing system.

10.5. The general principles of the data protection directive

Processing of gender information is governed by the general principles of the Directive. The main principle laid down by the Directive is that personal data must be processed fairly and lawfully and can only be collected for *specific, explicit and legitimate* purposes and not further processed in a way incompatible with those purposes (the so-called *finalité* principle).[78]

Under Article 8(7) of the Data Protection Directive from 1995[79] Member States shall determine the conditions under which a national identification number or any other identifier of general application may be processed.

---

[78] Article 6 of the directive provides:
1. Member States shall provide that personal data must be:
(a) processed fairly and lawfully;
(b) collected for specified, explicit and legitimate purposes and not further processed in a way incompatible with those purposes. Further processing of data for historical, statistical or scientific purposes shall not be considered as incompatible provided that Member States provide appropriate safeguards;
(c) adequate, relevant and not excessive in relation to the purposes for which they are collected and/or further processed;
(d) accurate and, where necessary, kept up to date; every reasonable step must be taken to ensure that data which are inaccurate or incomplete, having regard to the purposes for which they were collected or for which they are further processed, are erased or rectified;
(e) kept in a form which permits identification of data subjects for no longer than is necessary for the purposes for which the data were collected or for which they are further processed. Member States shall lay down appropriate safeguards for personal data stored for longer periods for historical, statistical or scientific use.

[79] 1995/46/EC.

10.6. Gender related problems

Questions relating to the lawfulness or otherwise of processing gender related data when contracting have only received scant attention[80] even though EU actors as set out in Chapter 3 have wide-ranging gender mainstreaming duties and information about gender is collected on a large scale by businesses, not least in e-business The Data protection Working Party set up in accordance with art 29 of the Data Protection Directive[81] briefly mentions gender in the Working Document. Privacy on the Internet - An integrated EU Approach to On-line Data from 2000 where it is stated (emphasis added):[82]

> A general rule is that in order to access a chat room, a detailed identification list is completed at the request of the Internet Service Provider, which usually includes the e-mail address, birth date, country, *sex* and sometimes certain preferencies of the person. ....
> These data can be collected and further processed for different purposes, such as *direct marketing*, but also *credit rating*, or *selling the data to insurance companies or employers.*

The interaction of contract law and data protection law is touched upon in the data protection directive and dealt with in books on protection of consumer data[83] but the interaction of contract law, data protection law and discrimination law is by and large passed over in silence in Europe.[84]

Collection and use of personal data by businesses may entail various risks such as privacy intrusions and covert forms of sex discrimination.

---

[80] Froomkin, A. Michael: Anonymity in the Balance, available at http://personal.law.miami.edu/~froomkin/ briefly mentions the advantages of gender anonymity.

[81] 95/46/EC.

[82] http://europa.eu.int/comm/internal_market/privacy/docs/wpdocs/2000/wp37en.pdf.

[83] See for example on Danish law in this field Blume, Peter og Mette Reissmann: Beskyttelse af forbrugeroplysninger, København 2003.

[84] See in respect of US law Ann Bartow: Our Data, Ourselves: Privacy, Propertization, and Gender, University of San Francisco Law Reviw 2000 p 633, Ann Bartow, Woman as Targets: The Gender-Based Implications of Online Consumer Profiling, Comment P994809, Federal Trade Commission Online Profiling Workshop, available at http://www.ftc.gov/bcp/workshops/profiling/comments/bartow.htm Bygrave, Lee: Data protection law - approaching its rationale, logic and limits, Dordrecht, 2002 discusses the ability of data protection law to control profiling in detail and points to the interaction of profiling and discrimination. His analysis is not related to contract law.

It is obvious that the Data Protection Directive[85] protects the privacy of both men and women.

10.6.1. Is gender information sensitive data?

The Directive offers a particularly high level of privacy protection for special categories of data by, as the main rule, prohibiting the processing of personal data revealing racial or ethnic origin, political opinions, religious or philosophical beliefs, trade-union membership, and the processing of data concerning health or sex life.

Data revealing information about a person's gender is not included in the above list.[86] The information that an identifiable person is either male or female can therefore not normally be regarded as a particularly sensitive data.

Data revealing that an identifiable woman is pregnant may be protected as data concerning health.

Data revealing that an identifiable woman belongs to a sub-group, for example single mothers who are particularly exposed to discrimination are not specially protected as the law stands at present.

10.6.2. Is gender profiling unlawful direct or indirect sex discrimination?

Gender profiles can be used in a way that amounts to direct or indirect sex discrimination as defined in existing gender equality legislation at antional level and in the proposed Directive on equal treatment in the provision of goods and services by subjecting individuals to group treatment.

As mentioned earlier one of the respondents in an analysis by the Danish Agency for Trade and Industry stated[87] that single mothers do not have much chance of obtaining a loan for their enterprises. The proposed Directive on equal treatment in the provision of goods and services explicitly classifies less favourable treatment of women for reasons of pregnancy and maternity as direct discrimination. If gender-biased assumptions - eg that it is bad business to grant commercial loans to single mothers - are used as basis for generating a profile the generation of the profile will in itself be an unlawful business practice even if not individual victims who have suffered discrimination can be found.

---

[85] 95/46/EC.

[86] See for details Article 8 of the Directive.

[87] The Relations of Banks to Women Entrepreneurs. The Analysis of the Danish Agency for Trade and Industry: Women Entrepreneurs Now and in the Future, Published by the Danish Agency for Trade and Industry, September 2000, available online at http://www.efs.dk/publikationer/rapporter/bankers.uk/index-eng.html. The quotation on single mothers is from part 2.2. The respondents in the analysis were staff in the banks and independant advisors to the banks, eg chartered accountants.

The existing data protection laws protect only against few aspects of profiling.[88] Article 15 of the data protection directive provides that Member States shall grant the right to every person not to be subject to a decision which produces legal effects concerning him or significantly affects him and which is based solely on automated processing of data intended to evaluate certain personal aspects relating to him, such as his performance at work, creditworthiness, reliability, conduct, etc. Member States shall provide that a person may be subjected to a decision of the kind referred to above if that decision:

> (a) is taken in the course of the entering into or performance of a contract, provided the request for the entering into or the performance of the contract, lodged by the data subject, has been satisfied or that there are suitable measures to safeguard his legitimate interests, such as arrangements allowing him to put his point of view; or
> (b) is authorized by a law which also lays down measures to safeguard the data subject's legitimate interests.

This provision restricts a particular application of a particular type of profiling process. It does not directly restrict the creation of profiles.

---

[88] See further Bygrave, Lee: Data protection law - approaching its rationale, logic and limits, Dordrecht, 2002 p 319 et seq.

Chapter 5

Remedies and Enforcement

1. Introduction

Judicial protection both at European and national level has been a much debated issue during recent years.[1] The ECJ stated in *Johnston*[2] that all persons have the right to obtain an effective remedy in a competent court against measures which they consider to be contrary to the principle of equal treatment for men and women.

In this Chapter, I discuss the interaction of contract law with the general EU requirements concerning remedies and enforcement as they have been interpreted by the ECJ in matters of gender equality and with the gender specific requirements in Articles 7, 8 and 11 of the proposed Article 13 Directive[3] on equal treatment in the provision of goods and services.

2. National Autonomy to Choose Remedies and Procedures

According to settled case-law, in the absence of EU rules governing the matter, it is for the domestic legal system of each Member State to designate the courts and tribunals having jurisdiction, to lay down the detailed procedural rules governing actions for safeguarding rights which individuals derive from Community law, and to choose the relevant remedies.[4]

---

[1] See Tridimas, Takis: The general principles of EC law, Oxford 1999, Van Gerven, Walter: Of Rights, Remedies and Procedures, Common Market Law Review 2000 p 501 and O'Keeffe, David and Bavasso, Antonio (eds): Judicial Review in European Union Law, The Hague 2000.

[2] Case 222/84, *Johnston* [1986] ECR 1651.

[3] COM(2003)657, Proposal for a Council Directive implementing the principle of equal treatment between women and men in the access to and supply of goods and services. SEC(2003)1213, Commission Staff Working Paper contains an Extended Impact Assessment of the proposal.

[4] See, in particular, Case 33/76 *Rewe* [1976] ECR 1989, paragraph 5; Case 45/76 *Comet* [1976] ECR 2043, paragraph 13; Case 68/79 *Just* [1980] ECR 501, paragraph 25; Case 199/82 *San Giorgio* [1983] ECR 3595, paragraph 12; Case C-208/90

The choice of penalties thus remains within the discretion of the Member States but their choice must be exercised with respect for the general EU law principles of equivalence, effectiveness and proportionality. In 1989, in *Commission* v *Greece*[5] the ECJ laid down some minimum Community conditions to be applied to the national rules. First, conditions attached to the national rules must not be less favourable than those attached to similar national actions. Second, the national rules must not be framed so as to render virtually impossible the exercise of Community rights. In any event, the remedy must be effective, proportionate and dissuasive.

Article II-47[6] of the draft Constitutional Treaty provides for a right to an effective remedy and to a fair trial before a tribunal (tribunal in French, Gericht in German). The first paragraph of Article II-47 is based on Article 13 ECHR[7] The second paragraph of Article II-47 corresponds to Article 6(1) ECHR but goes a little further in that it also covers public law, see below in part 7.[8] The

---

Emmott [1991] ECR I-4269, paragraph 16; Case C-312/93 *Peterbroeck* [1995] ECR I-4599, paragraph 12; Joined Cases C-430/93 and C-431/93 *Van Schijndel and Van Veen* [1995] ECR I-4705, paragraph 17; Case C-261/95 *Palmisani* [1997] ECR I-4025, paragraph 27; Case C-90/94 *Haahr Petroleum* [1997] ECR I-4085, paragraph 46; Case C-188/95 *Fantask and Others* [1997] ECR I-6783, paragraph 47; Case C-326/96 *Levez* [1998] ECR I-7835, paragraph 18, Case C-78/98 *Preston* [2000] ECR ECR I-3201 paragraph 31.

5   Case C-68/88 *Commission* v *Greece* [1989] ECR 2979.

6   Article II-47 of the draft Constitutional Treaty which incorporates the corresponding provision in the Charter of Fundamental rights reads:
     Everyone whose rights and freedoms guaranteed by the law of the Union are violated has the right to an effective remedy before a tribunal in compliance with the conditions laid down in this Article.
     Everyone is entitled to a fair and public hearing within a reasonable time by an independent and impartial tribunal previously established by law. Everyone shall have the possibility of being advised, defended and represented.
     Legal aid shall be made available to those who lack sufficient resources insofar as such aid is necessary to ensure effective access to justice.

7   Article 13 ECHR reads: Everyone whose rights and freedoms as set forth in this Convention are violated shall have an effective remedy before a national authority notwithstanding that the violation has been committed by persons acting in an official capacity.

8   Article 6 ECHR reads: In the determination of his civil rights and obligations or of any criminal charge against him, everyone is entitled to a fair and public hearing within a reasonable time by an independent and impartial tribunal established by law. Judgment shall be pronounced publicly....

ECJ has referred to Articles 6 and 13 ECHR as expressions of underlying general principles of Community law in *Johnston* and a number of subsequent judgments. Article II-47 applies to the institutions of the EU and of the Member States when they are acting in the sphere of EU law.

Under the *acquis communautaire* Member States are as set out above in Chapter 2 bound by the fundamental rights including for example the fundamental right not to be discriminated against on grounds of sex when they act within the sphere of Community law as for example within the scope of one of the contract law directives. It follows, for example, that the Directive on unfair terms in consumer contracts[9] makes sex discriminatory contractual terms unlawful and harassment and sexual harassment in the provision of goods and services are unlawful within the field of the Directive on doorstep selling.[10] A person who can only rely on the fundamental right not to be discriminated against on grounds of sex is, however, in a fairly weak position if she wants to enforce her right. If a door-step seller for example harasses a customer in her home the Directive on doorstep selling provides for no specific remedy but the national courts must follow the general principles of Community law and find an effective remedy. The appropriate remedy depends on the circumstances. Remedies may include: a declaration of rights, damages, an injunction ordering a party not to do something or to do something.[11]

In addition to the above general principles, which apply in all matters governed by Community law, Member States will be required to comply with the specific requirements provided for in Articles 7, 8 and 11 of the proposed Directive on equal treatment in the access to and supply of goods and services when (and if) that Directive is adopted. Those Articles lay down provisions on judicial and administrative procedures, compensation or reparation, legal standing, dialogue with organisations, time limits, burden of proof and specific equality bodies to control that the principle of equal treatment is observed.

2.1. The principle of proportionality

In *Colson*,[12] AG Rozes argued that the deterrent effect of the sanctions must be assessed on the basis of the principle of proportionality and compared to sanctions imposed in national law to other offences of the same gravity. The ECJ held that it is impossible to establish real equality of opportunity without an

---

[9] 93/13/EEC.

[10] 85/577/EEC.

[11] See eg the UK SDA Section 66(2) SDA.

[12] Case 14/83, *Colson* [1984] ECR 1891.

appropriate system of sanctions. Although full implementation of the employment directives does not require any specific form of sanction, it does entail that that sanction be such as to guarantee real and effective judicial protection. Moreover it must also have a real deterrent effect on the employer.

2.2. The principle of effectiveness

The classic formulation of the principle of effectiveness was introduced in *Comet*.[13] Where Community legislation does not specifically provide any penalty for an infringement or refers for that purpose to national laws, regulations and administrative provisions, Article 10 EC requires the Member States to take all measures necessary to guarantee the application and effectiveness of Community law. For that purpose, whilst the choice of penalties remains within their discretion, they must ensure that infringements of Community law are penalized under conditions, both procedural and substantive, which are analogous to those applicable to infringements of national law of a similar nature and importance and which, in any event, make the penalty effective, proportionate and dissuasive.[14]

In *Heylens*[15] the ECJ found that there must be a remedy of a judicial nature against the refusal of the French Minister to recognize a diploma. The Court held that since free access to employment is a fundamental right which the EC Treaty confers individually on each worker in the community, the existence of a remedy of a judicial nature against any decision of a national authority refusing the benefit of that right is essential in order to secure for the individual effective protection for his right. As the ECJ held in *Johnston* that requirement reflects a general principle of community law which underlies the constitutional traditions Common to the member states and has been enshrined in articles 6 and 13 ECHR.

In *Colson*,[16] the ECJ struck down a German rule providing for reliance damages as insufficient to deter employers from discriminating on grounds of sex, see for more details below on reliance damages.

---

[13] Case 45/76 Comet v Produktschap voor Siergewassen [1976] ECR 2043 and Case 33/76 Rewe-Zentral Finanz eG v Landwirtschaftskammer für das Saarland [1976] ECR 1989.

[14] See, for example, Case C-326/88 *Anklagemyndigheden* v *Hansen & Søn I/S* [1990] ECR I-2911.

[15] Case 222/86 *Heylens* [1987] ECR 4097.

[16] Case 14/83, *Colson* [1984] ECR 1891.

2.3. The principles of equivalence

The infringement actions[17] against UK for failure to implement the original collective redundancies and transfer of undertakings directives addressed the problem that employee representation in undertakings within the UK was based on voluntary recognition of trade unions by employers and for that reason there was no remedy against an employer who did not recognize a trade union. The ECJ considered this state of law incompatible with the duty of the Member States to contribute to the effective application of Community law. In this case the UK treatment of information and consultation of employees in matters covered by Community law was the same as the treatment of information and consultation of employees in national matters not covered by Community law, namely a totally voluntary solution. The principle of equivalence was thus fulfilled but the principle of effectiveness was violated.

3. Specific Performance

If a party does not perform a contract although performance is possible, the question arises whether the other party may claim performance in natura.

In *Colson*[18] the Arbeitsgericht Hamm raised the question as to whether the Equal treatment Directive[19] requires discrimination on grounds of sex in the matter of access to employment to be penalized by an obligation, imposed on an employer who is guilty of discrimination, to conclude a contract of employment with the candidate who was the victim of discrimination. The ECJ held that the Equal treatment Directive does not require discrimination on grounds of sex regarding access to employment to be made the subject of a sanction by way of an obligation imposed upon the employer who is the author of the discrimination to conclude a contract of employment with the candidate discriminated against.

In respect of specific performance employment contracts are special because of the personal character of the contract. In discrimination cases outside of the labour market the general rules in the national system which is the applicable law of the contract must apply. Under common law, the main rule is that there is no claim for specific performance. However, specific performance is granted if the normal sanction of damages would be inadequate. In civil law countries, the main rule is the opposite, namely that there is a claim for specific performance.

---

[17] Case C-382/92, *Commission* v *United Kingdom* [1994] ECR I-2435 and Case C-383/92, *Commission* v *United Kingdom* [1994] ECR I-2479.

[18] Case 14/83, *Colson* [1984] ECR 1891.

[19] 76/207/EEC.

4. Compensation or Reparation

Damages/compensation is a typical remedy in national law.[20] In discrimination cases in the employment field a number of questions have been raised as to which elements must be included.

4.1. The proposed directive

Article 7(2) in the the proposed directive on equal treatment in the provision of goods and services provides:

> 2. Member States shall introduce into their national legal systems such measures as are necessary to ensure real and effective compensation or reparation, as the Member States so determine, for the loss and damage sustained by a person injured as a result of discrimination within the meaning of this Directive, in a way which is dissuasive and proportionate to the damage suffered. Such compensation or reparation shall not be restricted by the fixing of a prior upper limit.

It is in broad terms similar to Article 6(2) of the amended equal treatment directive[21] which provides:

> 2. Member States shall introduce into their national legal systems such measures as are necessary to ensure real and effective compensation or reparation as the Member States so determine for the loss and damage sustained by a person injured as a result of discrimination contrary to Article 3, in a way which is dissuasive and proportionate to the damage suffered; such compensation or reparation may not be restricted by the fixing of a prior upper limit, except in cases where the employer can prove that the only damage suffered by an applicant as a result of discrimination within the meaning of this Directive is the refusal to take his/her job application into consideration.

To the difference of the proposed directive on goods and services the amended equal treatment directive explicitly states that the compensation or reparation that is ensured must be dissuasive and proportionate to the damage suffered. That applies also in respect of the proposed directive on goods and services since it follows from the general principles of EU law.

---

[20] See Bussani, Mauro (ed): Pure Economic Loss in Europe, Cambridge 2003 is a contribution to the common core project, see above in Chapter 2.

[21] 2002/73/EC.

4.2. Requirement of fault

In *Dekker*[22] the Hoge Raad (the Dutch Supreme Court) referred the question whether it is compatible with the Equal Treatment Directive that, if the infringement of the principle of equal treatment is established, for the award of the claim it is also necessary that the employer has committed a fault.

The ECJ held that the refusal to engage a pregnant woman on the ground that she is pregnant constitutes a form of direct discrimination on the grounds of sex. Furthermore, proof of such discrimination is not contingent upon a comparison with the treatment of a male employee. The ECJ stressed that the primary liability for a breach of the Equal Treatment Directive is upon the employer and that he or she cannot rely upon exemptions, exclusions or justifications available in national law to justify discrimination against a pregnant employee.

In *Draempaehl*,[23] the ECJ again discussed the question as to whether a requirement of fault in national law is consistent with EU law. The following preliminary question was referred to it:

1. Does a statutory provision which makes it a condition for an award of compensation for discrimination on grounds of sex in the making of an appointment that there must be fault on the part of the employer conflict with Articles 2(1) and 3(1) of Council Directive 76/207/EEC of 9 February 1976 on the implementation of the principle of equal treatment of men and women as regards access to employment, vocational training and promotion, and working conditions?

The Court referred to its judgment in *Dekker* and concluded that the equal treatment directive precludes provisions of domestic law which, like §611a(1) and (2) of the BGB, make reparation of damage suffered as a result of discrimination on grounds of sex in the making of an appointment subject to the requirement of fault. That conclusion could not be affected by the German Government's argument that proof of such fault is easy to adduce since, in German law, fault entails liability for deliberate or negligent acts.

The above rule on no-fault liability will probably correspondingly to sex discrimination outside of employment. In existing national law there are, however, examples of stricter liability rules in the employment field than outside of employment. The Norwegian Gender Equality Act Section 17 on liability for damages thus provides:

---

[22] Case C-177/88, *Dekker* [1990] ECR I-3941.

[23] Case C 180/95, *Draempaehl* [1997] ECR I 2195.

Any job seeker or employee who has been subjected to differential treatment in contravention of sections 3 to 6 shall be entitled to compensation regardless of the fault of the employer. Compensation shall be fixed at the amount that is reasonable, having regard to the financial loss, the situation of the employer and the employee or job seeker and all other circumstances.

In all other respects, the general rules regarding liability for damages in the event of wilful or negligent contravention of the provisions of this Act shall apply.

Similarly, in the UK damages cannot be awarded for indirect discrimination in the provision of goods and services under the UK SDA[24] if the respondent proves that the requirement or condition in question was not applied with the *intention* of treating the claimant unfavourably on the ground of his or her sex. The requirement of intention as a precondition for damages makes the UK ban against indirect discrimination in matters of goods and services weak compared to the standard provided for in employment and in the proposed Directive on equal treatment in contracts for the provision of goods and services.

4.3. Reliance damages

Reliance damages restore the injured party to his or her original pre-contractual position. Job-seekers whose right are violated, eg by discrimination, will often have incurred only limited economic loss such as the costs of stamps and an envelope. A duty to pay compensation for such costs will not be effective in deterring employers from discriminating.

In *Colson*[25] the ECJ ruled in a case where rejected applicants under German law received reimbursement of their application costs and nothing more. The Commission considered that although the directive is intended to leave to Member States the choice and the determination of the sanctions, the transposition of the directive must nevertheless produce effective results. The principle of the effective transposition of the directive requires that the sanctions must be of such a nature as to constitute appropriate compensation for the candidate discriminated against and for the employer a means of pressure which it would be unwise to disregard and which would prompt him to respect the principle of equal treatment. A national measure which provides for compensation only for losses actually incurred through reliance on an expectation (Vertrauensschaden) is not sufficient to ensure compliance with that principle.

The ECJ held that national provisions limiting the right to compensation of persons who have been discriminated against as regards access to employment to a purely nominal amount, such as, for example, the reimbursement of

---

[24] See further section 66 SDA.

[25] Case 14/83, *Colson* [1984] ECR 1891.

expenses incurred by them in submitting their application, would not satisfy the requirements of an effective transposition of the Equal Treatment Directive.

4.4. Upper limit for compensation and exclusion of interest

The question as to whether the Member States can put a ceiling on compensation was at issue both in *Marshall*[26] and in *Draempaehl*.[27]

Miss Marshall was dismissed in 1980 at the age of 62, in a situation in which a man would have been dismissed at the age of 65. In *Marshall* (1),[28] the ECJ ruled that this was in conflict with article 5 of the Directive on Equal Treatment,[29] which created direct effects *vis-à-vis* a public employer. Marshall then made a claim for compensation.

The dispute in *Marshall* (2)[30] arose because the Industrial Tribunal,[31] to which the Court of Appeal remitted the case to consider the question of compensation, assessed Miss Marshall' s financial loss at 18.405£, including 7.710 £ by way of interest, and awarded her compensation of 19.405 £, including a sum of 1.000£ compensation for injury to feelings. According to the then relevant provision of the SDA, where an Industrial Tribunal found that a complaint of unlawful sex discrimination in relation to employment was well founded, it should, if it considered it just and equitable to do so, make an order requiring the respondent to pay to the complainant compensation of an amount corresponding to any damages he could have been ordered by a County Court to pay to the complainant. Under the then section 65(2) of the SDA, however, the amount of compensation awarded could not exceed a specified limit, which at the relevant time was 6.250 £. At that time an Industrial Tribunal had no power - or at least the relevant provisions were ambiguous as to whether it had such a power - to award interest on compensation for an act of unlawful sex discrimination in relation to employment. The House of Lords referred a number of questions to the ECJ concerning the extent to which these restrictions complied with Article 6 of the Directive on Equal Treatment:

---

[26] Case C-271/91, *Marshall (No 2)* [1993] ECR I-4367.

[27] Case C-180/95, *Draempaehl* [1997] ECR I-2195.

[28] Case 152/84, *Marshall (1)* [1986] ECR 723.

[29] 76/207/EEC.

[30] Case C-271/91, *Marshall (No 2)* [1993] ECR I-4367.

[31] The then competent English tribunal, today it would be an employment tribunal.

1. Where the national legislation of a Member State provides for the payment of compensation as one remedy available by judicial process to a person who has been subjected to unlawful discrimination of a kind prohibited by Council Directive 76/207/EEC is the Member State guilty of a failure to implement Article 6 of the Directive by reason of the imposition by the legislation of an upper limit on the amount of compensation recoverable by such a person?

2. Where the national legislation provides for the payment of compensation is it essential to the due implementation of Article 6 of the Directive that the compensation to be awarded:

a) should not be less than the amount of the loss found to have been sustained by reason of the unlawful discrimination

b) should include an award of interest on the principal amount of the loss so found from the date of the unlawful discrimination to the date when the compensation is paid?

The ECJ understood the questions put by the House of Lords as asking, in essence, whether it follows from the Directive on Equal Treatment that a victim of sex discrimination is entitled to (emphasis added) *full reparation for the loss and damage he or she had sustained.*

The Court held that although the Equal Treatment Directive leaves Member States, when providing a remedy for breach of the prohibition against discrimination, free to choose between the different solutions suitable for achieving the objective of the directive, it nevertheless entails that if financial compensation is to be awarded where there has been discrimination such compensation must be adequate, in that it must enable the loss and damage actually sustained as a result of the discriminatory dismissal to be made good in full in accordance with the applicable national rules. Accordingly, the interpretation of Article 6 of the Equal Treatment Directive must be that reparation of the loss and damage sustained by a person injured as a result of discriminatory dismissal may not be limited to an upper limit fixed a priori or by excluding an award of interest to compensate for the loss sustained by the recipient of the compensation as a result of the effluxion of time until the capital sum awarded is actually paid. The response of the ECJ was that Article 6 should be interpreted such that damages for a loss, suffered by a person in the context of a dismissal which is discriminatory on the basis of gender, may not be restricted to a maximum amount determined *a priori*, and that interest must be awarded as compensation for a justified loss, in respect of the time elapsed until the damages are actually paid.

In *Draempaehl*[32] the national court referred questions for a preliminary ruling on whether it is in conflict with the Equal Treatment Directive that a statutory provision prescribes an upper limit of three months' salary as compensation for discrimination on grounds of sex in the making of an

---

[32] Case C-180/95, *Draempaehl* [1997] ECR I-2195.

appointment - in contrast to other provisions of domestic civil and labour law - for applicants of either sex who have been discriminated against in the procedure, but who would not have obtained the position to be filled even in the event of non-discriminatory selection by reason of the superior qualifications of the applicant appointed.

The national court also asked if a statutory provision is in conflict with the Equal Treatment Directive if it prescribes an upper limit of three month's salary as compensation for discrimination on grounds of sex in the making of an appointment - in contrast to other domestic provisions of civil and labour law - for applicants of either sex who, in the event of non-discriminatory selection, would have obtained the position to be filled. Finally it asked whether it is in conflict with the Equal treatment Directive if a statutory provision, where compensation is claimed by several parties for discrimination on grounds of sex in the making of an appointment, prescribes an upper limit of the aggregate of six months' salary for all persons who have suffered discrimination - in contrast to other provisions of domestic civil and labour law

The ECJ held that the Equal Treatment Directive does not preclude provisions of domestic law which prescribe an upper limit of three months' salary for the amount of compensation which may be claimed by an applicant where the employer can prove that, because the applicant engaged had superior qualification, the unsuccessful applicant would not have obtained the vacant position, even if there had been no discrimination in the selection process. In contrast, the Directive precludes provisions of domestic law which, unlike other provisions of domestic civil and labour law, prescribe an upper limit of three months' salary for the amou nt of compensation which may be claimed by an applicant discriminated against on grounds of sex in the making of an appointment where that applicant would have obtained the vacant position if the selection process had been carried out without discrimination.

Finally the ECJ held that the Directive precludes provisions of domestic law which, unlike other provisions of domestic civil and labour law, impose a ceiling of six months' salary on the aggregate amount of compensation which, where several applicants claim compensation, may be claimed by applicants who have been discriminated against on groun ds of their sex in the making of an appointment.

4.5. Compensation for non-material damage

In *Leitner*,[33] the ECJ was asked whether Article 5 of the package travel directive[34] is to be interpreted as meaning that compensation is in principle payable in respect of claims for compensation for non-material damage.

The Commission argued that the term damage is used in the Directive without any restriction, and that, specifically in the field of holiday travel, damage other than physical injury is a frequent occurrence. It then noted that liability for non-material damage is recognised in most Member States, over and above compensation for physical pain and suffering traditionally provided for in all legal systems, although the extent of that liability and the conditions under which it is incurred vary in detail. The Commission maintained that it is not possible to interpret restrictively the general concept of damage used in the Directive and to exclude from it as a matter of principle non-material damage.

The ECJ noted that it was not in dispute that, in the field of package holidays, the existence in some Member States but not in others of an obligation to provide compensation for non-material damage would cause significant distortions of competition, given that, as the Commission has pointed out, non-material damage is a frequent occurrence in that field. Furthermore, the Directive, and in particular Article 5 thereof, is designed to offer protection to consumers and, in connection with tourist holidays, compensation for non-material damage arising from the loss of enjoyment of the holiday is of particular importance to consumers. It is in light of those considerations that Article 5 of the Directive is to be interpreted.

Although the first subparagraph of Article 5(2) merely refers in a general manner to the concept of damage, the fact that the fourth subparagraph of Article 5(2) provides that Member States may, in the matter of damage other than personal injury, allow compensation to be limited under the contract provided that such limitation is not unreasonable, means that the Directive implicitly recognises the existence of a right to compensation for damage other than personal injury, including non-material damage. The answer to the question referred was therefore that Article 5 of the Directive is to be interpreted as conferring, in principle, on consumers a right to compensation for non-material damage resulting from the non-performance or improper performance of the services constituting a package holiday.

With regard to sex discrimination in the provision of goods and services national law also provide for compensation for non-material damage to a varying

---

[33]   Case C168/00, *Leitner* [2002] I-2631.

[34]   90/314/EEC.

160

degree.[35] The distortion of competition argument is probably weaker in this field than with regard to package holidays. The principle of effectiveness will often require compensation to be paid for non-material damage because there will typically be no physical injury and the economic loss sustained may be so small that compensation only for economic loss will not be sufficient for the sanction to act as a deterrent, see above on the *Colson* case.[36]

5. Courts

5.1. A fair and public hearing

Article II-47(2) of the draft Constitutional Treaty which incorporates the corresponding provision in Article 6 ECHR in the Charter of Fundamental rights reads:

> Everyone is entitled to a fair and public hearing within a reasonable time by an independent and impartial tribunal previously established by law. Everyone shall have the possibility of being advised, defended and represented.

5.1.1. Civil, criminal and public law
Article 6 ECHR has a more limited scope. It stipulates that in the determination of his civil rights and obligations or of any criminal charge against him, everyone is entitled to a fair and public hearing. Compared to that Article II-47(2) goes a little further.[37] In EU law, the right to a fair hearing is not confined to disputes relating to civil law rights and obligations and criminal proceedings but applies equally to public law. That is in the explanatory remarks seen as a

---

[35] See from national law section 66 (4) of the UK SDA which provides for compensation for injury to feelings.

[36] Case 14/83, *Colson* [1984] ECR 1891.

[37] Article 13 ECHR reads: In the determination of his civil rights and obligations or of any criminal charge against him, everyone is entitled to a fair and public hearing within a reasonable time by an independent and impartial tribunal established by law. Judgment shall be pronounced publicly but the press and public may be excluded from all or part of the trial in the interests of morals, public order or national security in a democratic society, where the interests of juveniles or the protection of the private life of the parties so require, or to the extent strictly necessary in the opinion of the court in special circumstances where publicity would prejudice the interests of justice.

consequence of the fact that the EU is a community based on the rule of law as stated by the ECJ in *Les Verts*.[38]

Contract law is in most EU countries looked upon as a core area of private law or civil law so that most parties to contracts will have a right to a fair trial both under Article 6 ECHR and Article II-47 of the draft EU Constitution. There is, however, in some countries (eg France) also a public law of contract in respect of contracts concluded by contracting authorities, for example in the context of public procurement. As discussed above in Chapter 4 there is some possibility of inserting equality clauses in invitations to tender. Litigation over such clauses will be protected by the draft Constitution irrespective of whether the problem is classified as a public law or a private law issue.

In all respects other than their scope, the guarantees afforded by the ECHR apply in a similar way to the EU.

5.1.2. Legal aid

Article II-47(3) of the draft Constitutional Treaty reads:

> Legal aid shall be made available to those who lack sufficient resources insofar as such aid is necessary to ensure effective access to justice.

This provision is in accordance with the case law of the ECtHR according to which provision should be made for legal aid where the absence of such aid would make it impossible to ensure an effective remedy.[39] In the explanatory remarks to the Charter of fundamental Rights this case law is mentioned as an example of the endeavors of the EU to live up to the standard established by ECHR.[40]

---

[38] Case 294/83, *Les Verts* [1988] ECR 1339.

[39] *Airey* v *Ireland*, judgment of 9.10.1979 in case no 6289/73, available at www.echr.coe.int/eng/Judgments.htm.

[40] Article 52(3) of the Charter provides: 'Insofar as this Charter contains rights which correspond to rights guaranteed by the Convention for the Protection of Human Rights and Fundamental Freedoms, the meaning and scope of those rights shall be the same as those laid down by the said Convention. This provision shall not prevent Union law providing more extensive protection.'

5.2. The proposed Directive on equal treatment in the provision of goods and services

Article 7 (1, 3 and 4) of the proposed Directive[41] on equal treatment in the access to and supply of goods and services contains under the heading 'Defence of rights' provisions on courts and procedures.[42] Article 7 relates to procedures (access to justice) which enable the obligations deriving fromthe Directive to be enforced.

5.3. An independent and impartial court

It is for the domestic legal system of each Member State to designate the courts and tribunals having jurisdiction. They can, however, not choose that no court or tribunal is competent. In *Commission* v *UK*[43] concerning the implementation of the Equal Pay Directive,[44] the ECJ thus held that each Member State must endow an authority with the requisite jurisdiction to decide whether work has the same value as other work

5.3.1. Gender composition of the courts and similar bodies
Malleson[45] argues that equal participation of men and women in the justice system is an inherent and essential feature of a democracy without which the judiciary will lose public confidence.

In the Danish gender equality Acts setting up the complaint board for equality thare is a gender parity. The board consists of three members among whihc both sexes must be reprsented. Presently two of the members are male and one female.

---

[41] COM(2003)756.

[42] Article 7 (1) reads: 1. Member States shall ensure that judicial and/or administrative procedures, including where they deem it appropriate conciliation procedures, for the enforcement of the obligations under this Directive are available to all persons who consider themselves wronged by failure to apply the principle of equal treatment to them, even after the relationship in which the discrimination is alleged to have occurred has ended.

[43] Case 61/81 *Commission* v *United Kingdom* [1982] ECR 2601.

[44] 75/117/EEC.

[45] Malleson, Kate: Justifying Gender Equality on the Bench: Why Difference Won't Do, Feminist Legal Studies 2003 p 1.

163

5.3.2. Competent court according to the regulation on jurisdiction and enforcement of judgements

Rules determining which national court is competent are providedfor in the Brussels Regulation on jurisdiction and the enforcement of judgements in civil and commercial matters.[46] This regulation establishes extra protection for employees and consumers. There are no special rules for discrimination cases.

5.4. Legal Standing - group action

Article 7(3) of the proposed Directive on equal treatment in the provision of goods and services provides that

> 3. Member States shall ensure that associations, organisations or other legal entities, which have, in accordance with the criteria laid down by their national law, a legitimate interest in ensuring that the provisions of this Directive are complied with, may engage, on behalf or in support of the complainant, with his or her approval, in any judicial and/or administrative procedur e provided for the enforcement of obligations under this Directive.

The right to legal protection is further reinforced by the possibility of allowing organisations to exercise such rights on behalf of a victim.

In the *Hejderijk* case[47] the ECJ indicated that the principles of effective judicial protection and effectiveness may lead to a 'locus standi' for a person who has no 'locus standi' under national law.

5.5. Time limits

5.5.1. The proposed Directive on equal treatment in the provision of goods and services

Article 7(1) of the proposed Directive on equal treatment in the provision of goods and services provides that (emphasis added):

> 1. Member States shall ensure that judicial and/or administrative procedures, including where they deem it appropriate conciliation procedures, for the enforcement of the obligations under this Directive are available to all persons who consider themselves wronged by failure to apply the principle of equal treatment to them *even after the relationship in which the discrimination is alleged to have occurred has ended.*

---

[46] EC/44/2001.

[47] Case C-89/90, *Verholen* [1991] ECR I-3757.

As in the earlier discrimination directives, the right to challenge discriminatory behaviour wiith regard to the provision of goods and services extends to situations in which the relationship between the parties has ended. In *Coote*,[48] the ECJ held that this follows from the principle of effective judicial control.

The proposed Directive will not get retroactive effect, applying to such relationships only from the date of its entry into force. National time limits for initiating action are not affected by this Article. Article 7(4) of the proposed Directive on equal treatment in the provision of goods and services provides that:

> 4. Paragraphs 1 and 3 are without prejudice to national rules on time limits for bringing actions relating to the principle of equal treatment.

5.5.2. *Case law of the ECJ*
National time-bars which may operate as hindrances to the effective enforcement of rights conferred upon individuals by EU law are usually adopted out of concern for the principle of legal certainty. When deciding as to whether to accept them it is therefore necessary to strike a balance between the conflicting general principles of legal certainty and of effectiveness.

In EU law in general the main rule is that national time-limits are considered to fall within the sphere of national procedural autonomy. The ECJ has thus recognised that it is compatible with Community law for national rules to prescribe, in the interests of legal certainty, reasonable limitation periods for bringing proceedings. It cannot be said that this makes the exercise of rights conferred by Community law either virtually impossible or excessively difficult, even though the expiry of such limitation periods entails by definition the rejection, wholly or in part, of the action brought.[49] In a few employment related situations time limits have, however, been struck down by the ECJ as incompatible with the principle of effectiveness inherent in EU law. In *Emmot*[50] the ECJ held that Community law precludes a Member State from relying, in proceedings brought against it by an individual before the national courts in order to protect rights directly conferred upon him by a directive, on national procedural rules relating to time-limits for bringing proceedings so long as that Member State has not properly transposed that directive into its domestic legal system. This -

---

[48] Case C-185/97, *Coote* [1998] ECR I-5199.

[49] See Case C-188/95, *Fantask and Others* [1997] ECR I-6783, Case C-326/96 *Levez* [1998] ECR I-7835 paragraph 19 and Case C-78/98, *Preston* [2000] ECR ECR I-3201.

[50] Case C-208/90, *Emmott* [1991] ECR I-4269.

seemingly far-reaching - ruling has been limited by later case law. In *Fantask*,[51] the ECJ stated that:

> the solution adopted in Emmott was justified by the particular circumstances of that case, in which the time-bar had the result of depriving the applicant of any opportunity whatever to rely on her right to equal treatment under a Community directive.

In *Magorrian & Cunningham*[52] the ECJ stated:

> 2. Community law precludes the application, to a claim based on Article 119 [now Article 141] of the EC Treaty for recognition of the claimants' entitlement to join an occupational pension scheme, of a national rule under which such entitlement, in the event of a successful claim, is limited to a period which starts to run from a point in time two years prior to commencement of proceedings in connection with the claim.

In *Preston and Fletcher*[53] the ECH confirmed its ruling in *Magorrian*.

5.6. Ex officio application of Community law

In *Océano*,[54] the ECJ held that the effectiveness of EU consumer protection legislation requires national courts to determine of their own motion whether a term of a contract is unfair with regard to the directive on unfair terms in consumer contracts.[55] The same principle must apply in discrimination cases.

6. Shift in the Burden of Proof

The ECJ has repeatedly stated[56] that it is normally for the person alleging facts in support of a claim to adduce proof of such facts. Thus, in principle, the burden of proving the existence of sex discrimination lies with the person who, believing him- or herself to be the victim of such discrimination, brings legal proceedings with a view to removing the discrimination.

---

[51] Case C-188/95 *Fantask* [1997] ECR I-6783.

[52] Case C-246/96, *Magorrian* [1997] ECR I-7153.

[53] Case C-78/98, *Preston* [2000] ECR ECR I-3201.

[54] Joined cases C-240/98 to C-244/98, *Océano Grupo Editorial* [2000] ECR I-4941.

[55] 93/13/EC.

[56] See for example Case C-127/ 92, *Enderby* [1993] ECR I-5535 paragraph 13.

In *Danfoss*,[57] the ECJ held (emphasis added) that the Equal Pay Directive[58] must be interpreted as meaning that where an undertaking applies a system of pay which is totally lacking in transparency, it is for the employer to prove that his *practice* in the matter of wages is not discriminatory, if a female worker establishes, in relation to a relatively large number of employees, that the average pay for women is less than that for men.

6.1. Indirect discrimination and lack of transparency

It is clear from the case-law of the ECJ that the onus may shift when that is necessary to avoid depriving workers who appear to be the victims of discrimination of any effective means of enforcing the principle of equal pay. Accordingly, when a measure distinguishing between employees on the basis of their hours of work has in practice an adverse impact on substantially more members of one or other sex, that measure must be regarded as contrary to the objective pursued by Article 141 EC, unless the employer shows that it is based on objectively justified factors unrelated to any discrimination on grounds of sex.[59]

Similarly, where an undertaking applies a system of pay which is wholly lacking in transparency, it is for the employer to prove that his practice in the matter of wages is not discriminatory, if a female worker establishes, in relation to a relatively large number of employees, that the average pay for women is less than that for men.[60] As stated in the Staff Working paper underlying the proposal for the Directive on equal treatment in the provision of goods and services[61] the example of sex discrimination reported include:

Refusal to offer loans to people working part-time.

Banks and other financial institutions which operate such practices will face the same consequences as to bruden of proof as employers have been met with in the above judgments.

---

[57] Case C-109/88, *Danfoss* [1989] ECR 3199.

[58] 75/117/EEC.

[59] Case 170/84, *Bilka-Kaufhaus* [1986] ECR 1607, at paragraph 31, Case C-33/89, *Kowalska* [1990] ECR I-2591, at paragraph 16, C-184/89, *Nimz* [1991] ECR I-297, at paragraph 15 and Case C-127/ 92,*Enderby* [1993] ECR I-5535 paragraph 13.

[60] Case 109/88, *Danfoss* [1989] ECR 3199, at paragraph 16.

[61] SEC(2003)1213 p 5.

6.2. Article 8 of the proposed Directive on equal treatment

Article 8[62] of the proposed Directive on equal treatment in the access to and supply of goods and services provides for a shift in the burden of proof to the advantage of persons who consider themselves wronged by a failure to apply the principle of equal treatment.

Article 8 of the proposed Directive is a standard provision in Community discrimination law. The wording is based on the Burden of Proof Directive[63] and the equivalent articles found in the earlier Article 13 Directives, notably the Directive on Race and Ethnic discrimination.[64] The burden of proof reverts to the respondent once the plaintiff has established facts before the court or other body from which it may be presumed that discrimination has taken place.

As in the earlier discrimination directives and in order to comply with the provisions of the ECHR, this shift in the burden of proof does not apply to situations where the criminal law is used to prosecute allegations of discrimination.[65]

---

[62] Article 8 reads: Burden of proof. 1. Member Statesshall take such measures as are necessary, in accordance with their national judicial systems, to ensure that, when persons who consider themselves wronged because the principle of equal treatment has not been applied to them establish,before a court or other competent authority, facts from which it may be presumed that there has been direct or indirect discrimination, it shall be for the respondent to prove that there has been no breach of the principle of equal treatment. 2. Paragraph 1 shall not prevent Member States from introducing rules of evidence which are more favourable to plaintiffs. 3. Paragraph 1 shall not apply to criminal procedures. 4. Paragraphs 1, 2 and 3 shall also apply to any proceedings brought in accordance with Article 7(3).

[63] Article 4 of Directive 97/80/EC on the burden of proof in sex discrimination cases covered by Article 141 ECand by Directives 75/117/EEC (equal pay), 76/207/EEC, amended by 2002/73 (equal treatment), and, insofar as discrimination based on sex is concerned, 92/85/EEC (pregnancy) and 96/34/EC (parental leave).

[64] 2000/43/EC.

[65] As in its earlier proposals, the Commission has not included the provision inserted by the Council in previous directives to the effect that Member States need not apply the shift of the burden of proof to proceedings in which it is for the courtor competent body to investigate the facts of the case. The Commission notes that there is considerable confusion about the meaning of this provision and believes that its inclusion would undermine the legal certainty of the article as a whole.

7. Promotion of dialogue with non-governmental organisations.

Article 10 of the proposed Directive on equal treatment in the access to and supply of goods and services provides:

> Dialogue with non-governmental organisations
> Member States shall engage in dialogue with appropriate non-governmental organisations which have, in accordance with their national law and practice, a legitimate interest in contributing to the fight against discrimination on grounds of sex with a view to promoting the principle of equal treatment.

8. Specific equality bodies

Article 11 of the proposed Directive on equal treatment in the access to and supply of goods and services provides:

> 1. Member States shall designate and make the necessary arrangements for a body or bodies for the promotion, analysis, monitoring and support of equal treatment of all persons without discrimination on the grounds of sex. These bodies may form part of agencies with responsibility at national level with the defence of human rights or the safeguard of individuals' rights, or bodies with responsibility for implementation of the principle of equal treatment for men and women as regards access to employment, vocational training and promotion, and working conditions.
> 2. Member States shall ensure that the competencies of the bodies referred to in paragraph 1 include:
> (a) without prejudice to the rights of victims and of associations, organisations or other legal entities referred to in Article 7(3), providing independent assistance to victims of discrimination in pursuing their complaints about discrimination;
> (b) conducting independent surveys concerning discrimination;
> (c) publishing independent reports and making recommendations on any issue relating to such discrimination.

As set out in Chaper 2 all EU countries have set up some kind of special equality machinery. In countries with specific gender equality legislation such bodies also have some powers to take part in legal enforcement. The proposed Directive lays down more precise provisions in this regard. It replicates the provisions of the Race Discrimination Directive[66] in as far as they deal with access to and supply of goods and services, and builds on the equivalent provision in the amended Equal Treatment Directive,[67] where the Member States are required to designate bodies to promote equal treatment for women and men

---

[66] 2000/43/EC.

[67] 2002/73/EC

in the labour market. It provides for a framework applicable to bodies at national level which would act independently to promote the principle of equal treatment. Member States may decide that these bodies would be the same as those provided for in the labour market field under Equal Treatment Directive and, as in that case, that they should be established at regional or local level provided that their whole territory is covered by such arrangements.

9. State Liability

The ECJ decided in 1991 in *Francovich*[68] that a Member State is in principle liable for harm caused to individuals by breaches of EU law, including the non-implementation of directives. The Court held that the right of a Member State to which a directive is addressed to choose among several possible means of achieving the result required by it does not preclude the possibility for individuals of enforcing before the national courts rights whose content can be determined sufficiently precisely on the basis of the provisions of the directive alone. There are no state liability cases which specifically deal with gender equality.

---

[68]   Joined Cases C-6/90 and C-9/90, *Francovich* [1991] ECR I-5357.

Bibliography

Allen, Cliff, Deborah Kania and Beth Yaeckel: One-to-One Web Marketing: Build a Relationship Marketing Strategy One Customer at a Time, 2nd Edition. New York, 2002

Alvizou, Anastasia A: Individual Tort Liability for Infringements of Community Law, Legal Issues of Economic Integration 2002 p 177

Andenæs, Mads og Wulf-Henning Roth (eds): Services and Free Movement in EU Law, Oxford 2002

Bartow, Ann: Woman as Targets: The Gender-Based Implications of Online Consumer Profiling, Comment P994809, Docket No 990811219-9219-01, Federal Trade Commission Online Profiling Workshop, November 8, 1999, available at http://www.ftc.gov/bcp/workshops/profiling/comments/bartow.htm

Bartow, Ann: Our Data, Ourselves: Privacy, Propertization, and Gender, University of San Francisco Law Reviw 2000 p 633

Basedow, Jürgen: The Renascence of Uniform Law, Europarättslig Tidskrift 1999 p 44

Basedow, Jürgen: The Case for a European Insurance Contract Code, Journal of Business Law 2001 p 569

Bell, Mark: Anti-discrimination law and the European Union, Oxford 2002

Bleckmann, Albert: Staatsrecht II - Die Grundrechte, München 1997

Blois, Keith and Sally Dibb: The Oxford Textbook of Marketing, Oxford 2000

Blume, Peter og Mette Reissmann: Beskyttelse af forbrugeroplysninger, København 2003

Blume, Peter: Protection of informational privacy, Copenhagen 2002

Brownsword, Roger: Individualism, Coopcrativism and an Ethic for European Contract Law, Moder Law Review 2001 p 628

Bussani, Mauro (ed): Pure Economic Loss in Europe, Cambridge 2003

Bygrave, Lee: Data protection law - approaching its rationale, logic and limits, Dordrecht, 2002

Conaghan, Joanne and Wade Mansell: The wrongs of tort, London 1999

Froomkin, A. Michael: Anonymity in the Balance, available at http://personal.law.miami.edu/~froomkin/

Geary, David: Notes on Family Guarantees in English and Scottish Law - A Comment, European Review of Private Law 2000 p 25.

Gerven, Walter van, Jeremy Lever, Pierre Larouche, Christian von Bar and Geneviève Viney: Torts - scope of protection. The common law of Europe casebooks, Oxford, 1999

Gordley, James: The enforceability of promises in European contract law, Cambridge 2001

Graver, Kjersti: Norwegian regulation on sex discriminatory advertising, in Krämer, Ludwig, Hans Micklitz and Hans Tonner(eds): Law and Diffuse Interests in the European Legal Order, Liber amicorum Norbert Reich, Baden-Baden 1997 p 429

Joerges, Christian: On the Legitimacy of Europeanising Europe's Private Law: Considerations on a Law of Justi(ce)-fication (justum facere) for the EU Multi-Level System, EUI Working Paper, Law 2003/3, http://hdl.handle.net/1814/198

Kenny, Mel: The 2003 action plan on European contract law: is the Commission running wild?, European Law review 2003 p 538

Krämer, Ludwig, Hans Micklitz and Hans Tonner(eds): Law and Diffuse Interests in the European Legal Order, Liber amicorum Norbert Reich, Baden-Baden 1997

Lando, Ole and Hugh Beale (eds): Principles of European Contract Law. Parts I and II, Prepared by the Commmission on European Contract Law, The Hague, London, Boston, Kluwer Law International 2000

Lando, Ole, Eric Clive, Andre Prum and Reinhard Zimmerman: Principles of European Contract Law. Part III, The Hague, London, Boston, Aspen Publishers 2003

Lemire, Beverly, Ruth Pearson and Gail Campbell (eds): Women and credit - Researching the past, refiguring the future, Oxford, 2002

Malleson , Kate: Justifying Gender Equality on the Bench: Why Difference Won't Do, Feminist Legal Studies 2003 p 1

Malmberg, Jonas (ed): Effective Enforcement of EC Labour Law, Uppsala 2003

Mancini, G: The Making of a Constitution for Europe, Common Market Law Review 1989 p 595.

McCrudden, Christopher: Equality in Law between Men and Women in the European Community, United Kingdom, Luxembourg 1994

Morris, Debra: Surety Wives in the House of Lords: Time for Solicitors to 'Get Real'? Royal Bank of Scotland plc v Etridge (No. 2) [2001] 4 All E.R. 449, Feminist Legal Studies 2003 p 57

Müller-Graff, Peter-Christian: Gemeinsames Privatrecht in der Europäischen Gemeinschaft, Baden-Baden 1999

Nielsen, Ruth: European Labour Law, DJØF Publishing 2000

Nielsen, Ruth: Gender Equality in European Contract Law - a response to COM(2003)68, A More Coherent European Contract Law - An Action Plan, at the Commission's contract law website http://europa.eu.int/comm/consumers/cons_int/safe_shop/fair_bus_pract/cont_law/stakeholders/5-37.pdf

Nielsen, Ruth: Gender Equality in European Contract Law, DJØF Publishing 2004

Oakley, Ann: Experiments in knowing - Gender and method in the social sciences, Oxford 2000

O'Leary, Siofra: Employment Law at the European Court of Justice. Judicial Structures, Policies and Processes, London 2002

Palmer, Adrian: Principles of Marketing, Oxford 2000

Prechal, Sacha: Community Law in National Courts: the Lessons from van Schijndel, Common Market Law Review 1998 p 681

Quinlan, Mary Lou: Just Ask a Woman - cracking the code of what women want and how they buy, New York 2003

Roseberry, Lynn: The Limits of Employment Discrimination Law in the United States and European Community, Copenhagen 1999

Schiek, Dagmar: Differenzierte Gerechtigkeit. Diskriminierungsschutz und Vertragsrecht, Baden-Baden 2000

Schiek, Dagmar: Torn between Arithmetic and Substantive Equality? Perspectives on Equality in German Labour Law, The International Journal of Comparative Labour Law and Industrial Relations 2002 p 149

Schulze, Reiner : The Acquis Communautaire and the Development of European Contract Law, www.uni-muenster.de/Jura.iwr/Schulze/Aktuelles/Schulze%20 englisch.pdf

Schulze, Reiner, Hans Schulte-Nölke and Jackie Jones: A casebook on European consumer law, Oxford 2002

Staudenmayer, Dirk: The Commission Action Plan on European Contract Law, European Review of Private Law 2003

SOU 2003:16, Mansdominans i förändring - om ledningsgrupper och styrelser

Tenancy Law Reports from the European Private Law Forum Project Tenancy Law and Procedure in the European Union at the EUI, http://www.iue.it/ LAW/Research Teaching/EuropeanPrivateLaw/Projects.shtml

The Relations of Banks to Women Entrepreneurs. The Analysis of The Danish Agency for Trade and Industry: Women Entrepreneurs now and in the Future,

Published by the Danish Agency for Trade and Industry September 2000, available online at http://www.efs.dk/publikationer/rapporter/bankers.uk/index-eng.html
Totten, Christopher D: Constitutional Precommitments to Gender Affirmative Action in the European Union, Germany, Canada and the United States: A Comparative Approach, Berkeley Journal of International Law, 2003 p 27
Tuori, Kaarlo: Towards a Multi-Layered View of Modern Law, in Aarnio, Aulis et al (eds): Justice, Morality and Society, Lund 1997
Tuori, Kaarlo: EC Law: An Independent Legal Order or a Post-Modern Jack-in-the-Box? in I. Cameron and A. Simoni (eds) Dealing with Integration, vol 2, Perspectives from seminars on European Law 1996-1998 p 225 et seq, Uppsala 1998
Tuori, Kaarlo: Critical Legal Positivism, Aldershot 2002

Warren, Elizabeth: What is a Women's Issue? Bankruptcy, Commercial Law, and Other Gender-Neutral Topics, Harvard Women's Law Journal, 2002 p 19
Whittaker, xx The Law Quarterly Review 2001 p 215

Wilhelmsson, Thomas: Critical Studies in Private Law - A Treatise on Need-Rational Principles in Modern Law, Kluwer, Deventer 1992.
Wilhelmsson, Thomas: Social Contract Law and European Integration, Dartmouth 1995
Wilhelmsson, Thomas: Private Law in the EU: Harmonised or Fragmented Europeanisation?, European Review of Private Law 2002 p 77

Zimmermann, Reinhard and Simon Whittaker (eds), Good Faith in European Contract Law, Cambridge 2000,
Zweigert, Konrad and Hein Kötz: An Introduction to Comparative Law, Oxford 1998